WHAT MAKES A MAN?

WHAT MAKES A MAN?

12 PROMISES THAT WILL CHANGE YOUR LIFE

BILL McCARTNEY

HEAD FOOTBALL COACH, COLORADO UNIVERSITY

—————————————— WITH ——————————————

▸Gary Smalley ▸John Trent, Ph.D.
▸Dr. Larry Crabb ▸Luis Palau ▸Leighton Ford
▸Dr. James Dobson ▸Bill Hybels ▸Steve Farrar
▸Jack Hayford ▸Dennis Rainey ▸And Others

NAVPRESS

BRINGING TRUTH TO LIFE
NavPress Publishing Group
P.O. Box 35001, Colorado Springs, Colorado 80935

Library of Congress Catalog Card Number: 92-61235
ISBN 08910-97074

Sixth printing, 1994

General Editor/Project Manager: Stephen Griffith
Typist and Administrative Assistant: Jenny Phillips
Editors included Steve Webb, Les Troyer, Bill Deckard,
    Jean Stephens, and Debby Weaver
Many thanks to: Steve Webb, Shelley Webb, Rick Kingham,
    John Trent, Tim Kimmel, and Debbie Fawcett and
    Elaine Griffith for her patience.

Scripture in the publication is from the *Holy Bible: New
International Version* (NIV), copyright © 1973, 1978, 1984,
International Bible Society, used by permission of
Zondervan Bible Publishers; the *New American Standard
Bible* (NASB), © The Lockman Foundation 1960, 1962, 1963,
1968, 1971, 1972,1973, 1975, 1977; the *Revised Standard
Version Bible* (RSV), copyright © 1946, 1952, 1971, by the
Division of Christian Education of the National Council of
Churches of Christ in the USA, used by permission, all rights
reserved; the *Good News Bible: Today's EnglishVersion* (TEV) Old
Testament © 1976 American Bible Society, New Testament
© 1966, 1971, 1976 American Bible Society; the *New King James
Version* (NKJV), copyright © 1979, 1980, 1982, Thomas
Nelson Inc., Publishers; and the *King James Version* (KJV).

Printed in the United States of America

PROMISE KEEPERS: This book is dedicated to all the men
who are endeavoring to be promise keepers. They are
the living proof that Promise Keepers is not just an
organization or ministry, but men looking for God's
guidance. For more information concerning the Promise
Keepers, turn to page 240.

The Navigators is an international Christian organization.
Jesus Christ gave His followers the Great Commission to go
and make disciples (Matthew 28:19). The aim of The
Navigators is to help fulfill that commission by multiplying
laborers for Christ in every nation.
    NavPress is the publishing ministry of The Navigators.
NavPress publications are tools to help Christians grow.
Although publications alone cannot make disciples or change
lives, they can help believers learn biblical discipleship, and
apply what they learn to their lives and ministry.

Contents

It's Time for Men to Take a Stand

Bill McCartney

Each one of us has a story to tell about how our life has unfolded. From the youngest little guy to the oldest man, there's a story that's threaded through our lives. I'd like to tell you some of my story—my testimony.

I grew up in the home of a godly family and was taught strong moral values. My dad saw to it that we went to church every Sunday, but it was just a case of going to church on Sunday. As I grew up, I began to notice that I could earn distinction and gain an identity for myself by my performance in athletics. I discovered that the better I performed, the more honors I earned, and the better I felt about myself. This "performance-oriented self-esteem" guided my first thirty-three years. I noticed that the times when my performance was really good, were the best times. When I was struggling or failing, it wasn't nearly as sweet. And through it all, there seemed to be a void, a vacuum, an emptiness as to what was the real purpose of my life.

SEARCHING FOR A PURPOSE IN LIFE THROUGH FOOTBALL

I got an opportunity to go to the University of Missouri on a football scholarship. I was so proud when they put that in the paper. I thought that everyone in Riverview, Michigan would realize that surely Bill McCartney has arrived and he's a guy that everyone can look to with respect and admiration. That was important to me. It wasn't long after I got to Missouri that I realized most of the guys there were every bit as talented, or more talented than I was. I knew if I was going to have their respect and admiration, I had to do something significant. At first, I just wanted to make the team. Then I wanted to get in the game. Then, that wasn't enough, I wanted to be a starter. Once I became a starter, I wanted to earn honors. You really couldn't satisfy me.

My attempts to earn self-esteem carried over into my coaching career. As a high school coach, I began to discover that the more games we won, the better I felt about myself and the better I was received in the community. That fueled an initiative that drove me long and hard trying to achieve and accomplish things as a coach. Then the really big break came.

At the age of thirty-three, in 1974, I got the opportunity to go to the University of Michigan and be on that great football staff. I was the only high school coach Bo Schembechler ever hired. That was important to me. I knew that once I walked into that big stadium of 100,000 and rubbed elbows with the winningest football coach in the country, everybody would recognize, once and for all, that Bill McCartney had arrived. But it wasn't long after I got there that I discovered everybody there knew more football than I did. I again realized that if I was going to get their attention, affection, or esteem, I would have to achieve great things.

Then I met Chuck Heater. I was thirty-three years old and there was a guy on our team who was nineteen. He was a sophomore, fullback-running back and I noticed a quality to his life, a dimension to him, that was very attractive to me. So, I approached him. I said, "Chuck Heater, I see in you a dimension that I know I don't have. You're such a great competitor. You're so fiery and yet there's a peace and a serenity to you that's so beautiful. What is it about you?" Chuck stood back for a second and sized me up. He wasn't used to being approached by a coach on the Michigan staff quite like that. He said, "I'll tell you what, Coach. In two weeks eighteen Michigan athletes from all sports are having a conference in Brighton, Michigan. I'd like for you to come. Then, I'll try to answer your question."

FINDING PURPOSE AT LAST

What I heard at that conference changed my life, and it has never been the same. For the first time I was confronted with whether or not I had actually surrendered control of my life to Jesus Christ. I understood that if I would submit to Christ, Almighty God would take dominion in my heart and take over the direction in my life. Then, my life would start to gain some real satisfaction and fulfillment. That really appealed to me because in my work I had just entered into an arena where it was extremely competitive and I wasn't feeling good about myself.

I remember going home that day being excited because I had made a decision to give my life to Jesus Christ. It was something I had never done before. My wife, Lyndee, was in the living room with a lady from the neighborhood. I came busting in the front door and told her what happened. I then excused myself and left the room. The neighbor reached over and tapped Lyndee in the ribs and said, "I've seen it before. Don't worry about it. It blows right over." But it didn't blow over.

One of the reasons it didn't blow over was because I immediately started getting together with other men—for encouragement, fellowship, prayer, and Bible study.

THE OPPORTUNITY BEFORE US

We have a unique opportunity today, the chance to stand up, be counted, and give men who have chosen a different road an alternative before it's too late. We need to recapture the spiritual climate in our own homes and cultivate a heart for other men. Our homes, men, are about to collapse. The homes we live in are coming apart at the seams. But we can't just worry about our own homes. We've got to foster regard and concern for the homes around us. Together we must stand up and be counted for Almighty God.

To accomplish all this, to till the rough ground of this hostile culture and plant some new seeds for Christ, each of us must commit to model what I call the three non-negotiables of manhood: integrity, commitment and action.

If you were to take the word integrity and reduce it to its simplest terms you'd conclude that a man of integrity is a promise keeper. He's a guy who, when he says something, can be trusted. When he gives his word, you can take it to the bank. His word is good.

Being a promise keeper is easier said than done. In an athletic contest we know beforehand the designated place and time for the competition. Our adversary is identified for us. We also know he wants to beat our butts as badly as possible and in front of as many people as possible. This contest of life is quite different. In life, our adversary sometimes "prowls like a roaring lion, looking for someone to devour." But other times, he masquerades as an "angel of light." We don't know when or where he's going to show up next. (Although in Colorado, we know he'll probably wear the Nebraska colors—red and white!) But truthfully, he really comes in many different shapes and forms. So, how do we prepare? How do we prepare for the adversary? Let me suggest one possibility.

PLAYING THE GAME FOR SOMEONE ELSE

As head football coach of the University of Colorado Buffaloes, I have an intense desire to beat our arch-rival, Nebraska every time we play them. Unfortunately, when we were facing them in 1991, we had not won when we played in Lincoln for twenty-three years. So, on Thursday night before the Nebraska game on Friday, I had the team together in one room, and I explained to our guys that I had heard somewhere that we spend 86 percent of our time thinking about ourselves and just 14 percent thinking about others. I then told them that if you could ever get a guy to stop thinking about himself and start thinking about others, there's a whole new energy source available to him. With that in mind, I said, "Men, I've ordered sixty footballs and we're going to put the final score of Saturday's game on these balls. On Monday, we're going to send each ball to a person you've designated in advance. Here's what I'm asking you to do. By midnight tonight, Thursday night, I'm requiring any guy who wants to get on that airplane to Nebraska to dedicate this game to somebody other than himself. I want you to call that person and tell him (or her) that he ought to watch you on every play. If he can't be at the game, then tell him to watch it on television. Tell him you are going to show how much you love him, that you're going to play with all your heart, and you're playing this game for him. It might be your mom or dad. I want you to call tonight. Then, I want you to demonstrate that love on Saturday."

Do you remember what happened in that game? The Colorado Buffaloes broke a twenty-three year losing streak in Lincoln and won the game 27-12.

Christian men all over our nation and around the world are suffering because they feel they are on a losing streak and they can't break the pattern. The Adversary has us where he wants us— feeling defeated. It need not be that way.

READ THIS BOOK FOR SOMEONE ELSE

This book, *What Makes a Man? Twelve Promises That Will Change Your Life,* is a men's get together in print. Sharing their problems, lessons learned, discoveries, etc., are men just like you and me, men trying to prepare themselves to be godly men, promise keepers, prepared for the ever-present conflict with the Adversary and his minions.

Before you dip into the treasures of this book, I challenge you to dedicate your time reading, to someone you love. Tell her (or him) you are going to show how much you love her, that you're going to read and study this book with all your heart, and that you're reading for her. It might be your wife, a friend, or Almighty God himself. I want you to tell her how much you love her. Then, I want you to demonstrate that love by learning what God has in store for you in the following pages.

God's eyes are moving to and fro for men with a full passion for the gospel message. The Lord is calling men from across our nation to lead a new uprising of men filled with God's Spirit. Now is the time for that uprising, and this book contains many of the voices who are calling men to this movement.

It is my prayer that this book will be a tool to encourage you, challenge you, and move you as you seek to be the kind of man Almighty God wants you to be.

1

What Are Promises?

Gary Smalley and John Trent

The wife of a not-too-distinguished writer once asked French author Francois Coppee to support her husband's candidacy for a place in the French Academy.

"I beg you, vote for my husband," she pleaded. "He says he'll die if he's not elected." Coppee agreed to help, but his vote failed to ensure the writer's success.

A few months later, another seat became vacant and the lady returned to Coppee to ask him to vote for her husband again.

"Ah, no," replied the academician. "I kept my promise but he did not keep his. I consider myself free of any obligation."

Promise keeping and promise breaking. Each one of us has known both keepers and breakers. And when we talk about promises, certain images immediately come to mind. We see:

•Douglas MacArthur leaving the Philippines and promising his soldiers and the world that, "I shall return."
•Babe Ruth pointing his bat to the bleachers, promising to hit one out of the park, and then triumphantly doing just that.
•And Christ, making the greatest promise of all, telling His disciples that "he must go to Jerusalem and suffer many things at the hands of the elders, chief priests and teachers of the law, and that he must be killed and on the third day be raised to life" (Matthew 16:21). The greatest of all promise keepers.

But we also know about promise breakers. Unfortunately, many of the well-known role models of this century are not promise keepers, and we have only to look in the mirror to find someone who has broken a promise. Each of us could undoubtedly tell stories of being deeply hurt by others who have not kept their word.

What is a promise? Webster defines it as, "to give a basis for hopes or expectations." A promise giver is one who gives a basis for hopes and expectations and a promise keeper is one who fulfills those hopes and expectations.

Each child comes into the world as a person with promise. We look at certain children and say, "There goes a promising prospect." A promise keeper is no longer a prospect, but the fulfillment of that prospect.

People are counting on you to be a promise keeper—your wife, family, friends, co-workers, neighbors, and fellow citizens. The burden of that responsibility may be taking its toll on you. Don't despair. Take heart. You can begin being a promise keeper today. It won't be easy because we do have an Adversary and our struggle is "not against flesh and blood, but against the rulers, against the authorities, against the powers of this dark world and against the spiritual forces of evil in the heavenly realms" (Ephesians 6:12). But despite the obstacles, the one thing we (who have chosen the straight and narrow path that leads to life) know is that our leader is Jesus Christ, the King of kings, and the Lord of lords.

And don't forget, promise keeping is not just a responsibility. There are two sides to each promise we make. One side of a promise is the responsibility of keeping the promise. This side defines us as either a promise keeper or a promise breaker. But the other side is equally important. Keeping your promise holds its own reward. There are great benefits in keeping your promise— the trust of others, self-confidence, and other positive consequences we'll discover as we journey through this book.

The key question now is, Do you consider yourself a promise breaker, a promising prospect, or a promise keeper? The two following articles look more closely at the primary role model we have as promise keepers—God Himself.

Defining a Promise Keeper

Leighton Ford

*Nothing binds us one to the other like a promise
kept and nothing divides us like a promise broken.*

The insurance ad with the above copy reflects a change in the theme music of our culture. In the eighties we heard people say, "I'm out of here. There's nothing in it for me." I believe that theme music is slowly changing. Now we're beginning to hear, "I'm in for the long haul. Count on me." At least, I pray it is changing.

Two years ago on New Year's my wife and I had the privilege of going to Miami for the Orange Bowl. At that time a friend of mine introduced me to Bill McCartney, the Colorado coach. We walked around the track about eight times before his practice on a Sunday afternoon. I had a nice conversation with him. I said, "Bill, I understand you like to walk."

McCartney replied, "I really enjoy it."

I then asked him, "What do you do? Do you plan the practice when you are walking?"

He immediately answered, "No, I pray when I'm walking."

"You do? That's interesting. Tell me about it," I said.

So he told me how he prayed and about some of his spiritual roots and a change that took place in his life at thirty-three years of age through the influence of a nineteen-year-old football player at Michigan.

Then I asked, "What is your number-one goal?" What he said has stuck with me to this day. He said, "We want to beat Notre Dame; and we want to be number one. But my real goal is to use what influence I have to help raise up a generation of promise keepers. I think we need people in our country who will be promise keepers—in our families, in our businesses, in our public life, in everything."

WHY BE A PROMISE KEEPER?

Promise keepers—that's been going over and over in my mind since then. Why do we make promises? Why do we keep promises? If the ship is sinking, why not jump ship? If the fun has gone out of the marriage, why not walk away? If the people who are closest to us are going through pain, why hang in there?

Ethics professor Dr. Lewis Smedes has said that our character depends on promise keeping. When you make a promise, whether it's to yourself or someone else, you are making an appointment with yourself at some point some time out there in the future. Will you show up for that appointment? Your character depends on it. And Dr. Smedes also points out that our future in a very real sense rides on promise keeping. Almost everything in our lives hangs on that single thread of keeping promises to one another. That's the only way an uncertain future gets some certainty about it.

Not only are our character and the future dependent on the keeping of promises, but God Himself is a promise keeper and you and I were made to be like Him.

I heard a story about a man who was having a hard time. His business was falling apart. His wife was leaving him because of the financial problems. He couldn't meet the mortgage payments on his house.

One day he is driving into work, and has an accident. Soon, a policeman is writing out a ticket and an ambulance is coming because the guy in the other car has been hurt. The businessman doesn't know if his insurance is up-to-date and he's had enough. He looks up and says, "God, why me?" And a big voice comes booming out of the sky and says, "Well, Sam, the truth is, there's something about you that just ticks me off."

Is that what God is like? Is He fickle? No. To me, the most impressive characteristic about the God of the Bible is that He is a God who makes covenants—promises—and He keeps them.

BIBLE SNAPSHOTS

The Old Testament

Abraham was an ordinary sheepherder. "Abraham," God says, "Go to another country and if you do what I say, I'll bless you." The moving van shows up. His friends ask, "Where are you going?"

Abraham answers, "I don't know."

"Got a map?"

"No."

"Who is going to meet you there?"

"God."

"How do you know?"

"He said He would."

God promised and God acted on that promise.

Then Moses through a burning bush hears God say, "I'm choosing you to lead my people."

Because Moses wants to get a better fix on who's speaking, he replies, "Wait a minute. What is your name?"

God answers, "My name is Yahweh," which could be literally translated, "I am the One who will be with you."

Moses and the Jewish people staked their future on that promise.

The children of Israel broke their promises many times but when they got to the Promised Land, as we call it, Joshua, Moses' successor, said, "Look, people, of all the good promises the Lord gave, not one has failed. He's a promise keeper."

The New Testament

Then we come to the New Testament. A Man from Galilee said to His friends two thousand years ago, "I am going to spill my blood to keep those ancient promises." And He did and He made a new promise. "I am the One who will be with you to the very end of the world."

Later, there was a Christ-follower whose name was Paul. Paul had made some plans to visit and help some people, and he had to change his plans for a very good reason. They said, "You can't depend on him. He says one thing and means another. He's not dependable."

How did Paul answer them? This is what he said:

"Do I make my plans in a worldly manner so that in the same breath I say 'yes, yes' and 'no, no'. As surely as God is dependable, our message to you is not yes and no for the Son of God. Jesus Christ was not 'yes' and 'no', but in Him it has always been 'yes'."

No matter how many promises God has made, they are "yes" in Christ. You can depend on it.

OUR FOUR BASIC NEEDS AS HUMAN BEINGS

A psychiatrist friend tells me we have four basic needs as human beings. We need love, forgiveness, purpose, and hope. Those four deepest needs, our most profound questions, God has answered in Jesus Christ. God, am I loved? Yes. Can I be forgiven, God? Yes. Is there purpose? Yes. Is there hope beyond the grave? To all these questions God has given an everlasting yes in Jesus Christ.

Promise keeping is what the Passover is all about. This is the week when, whether Jew or Christian, we remember that God said to Jewish people in Egypt, "When the judgment day comes, if you'll put some blood over the door posts, I will pass over and I won't harm you." And God followed through. For Christ's followers, this is the week when we remember that there was a promise of a Savior who would come and bring forgiveness and strength and hope, and who sealed that promise with His blood on Good Friday. On Easter Sunday his resurrection was a mighty amen, when God said once and for all emphatically, "I'm going to keep My promises."

The week before last I was having lunch with a fellow in Oakland, California—a man who has done me a good turn. He's going through a lot of pressures. His son has been on drugs, in prison for four years, and now on the streets. His wife has reverted to the emotional level of a twelve-year-old after both her parents committed suicide with the same gun. She literally saw her father blow the top of his head off. I awkwardly commented, "This is tough." He looked at me across the table and said, "Leighton, I was pouring all of this out to a friend of mine who just received a diagnosis of leukemia from Stanford Hospital. I said to this friend of mine, 'Life is a terminal illness.' My friend looked at me with a smile and said, 'Kevin, you are looking at Jesus from the wrong side of the cross. You are looking from the crucifixion side. Look from the resurrection side and you'll have a new perspective on life and death.'"

On the thread of promise everything hangs. Let me suggest three "yes" words that mark the promise keeper (suggested to me by my son, Kevin): *integrity*, *fidelity*, and *loyalty*.

INTEGRITY

Am I a promise keeper in my work? In our culture, ethics have almost become a joke. And yet, maybe something is surfacing, a renewed hunger for integrity. Did you watch Barbara Walters interview General Schwarzkopf? She asked, "General, did you lie about the body count in Vietnam?" He said, "Sure." He paused and then continued, "There was a terrible erosion in integrity in the armed forces during Vietnam. I don't think many of us could hold our heads up and say, 'My integrity is still really white and pure.' It did bad things to the officer corps. But it's a different corps today, a corps that has learned. And when we went into [the war with Iraq], I was bound and determined we were going to tell it like it was, absolutely tell it like it was." There was a hunger for integrity.

Charlie Olcott is a new member of the board for Leighton Ford Ministries, and he's a man who passed the mirror test. He was the president of one of the largest fast-food franchises in the country. Another company was trying to buy them out. The chairman of his company's board came and said, "Charlie, I want you to make some ten-year projections on our earnings at a higher sales level than we've originally planned." Charlie, a financial man, said he couldn't do it. "I could make them at the original level, but I couldn't estimate them at a higher level just to give the company a better sale price." Just before they were going into the meeting with the investment bankers, he told his chairman, "I've thought about it all night. I can't do it." The chairman said, "OK, Charlie, you're off the team." Twenty years of climbing the corporate ladder and he was fired. He called his wife, Suzanne, and said, "I've been fired." She said, "Good, come on home." He went home. That was two years ago. Although it hasn't been an easy two years, he can look in the mirror. He told me, "I learned it was wrong to park my Christ-centered life at noontime Sunday." He knew who he was—a man who was a promise keeper.

FIDELITY

Here's another key "yes" word for promise keepers—*fidelity*. Am I a promise keeper in my family? Do you remember when Bob Simon, the CBS correspondent, was released by the Iraqis after being held for forty days? When he was interviewed he was asked, "What did you think about?" He said, "You know what I thought about most? I thought about the time I took my little girl in my arms and for the first time walked into the surf of the Mediterranean with her. And I thought about when I courted my wife. Not journalism, not news, not history—those rare personal moments that made my life so good." And he said, "I wanted more."

What makes a marriage more than a contract, more than passion spilling over? What makes a family? A family is a lot more than the census bureau says, two or more people related by blood living under the same roof. A family and a marriage is a community created by promise, a people of promise.

My wife, Jeanie, and I were married thirty-seven years ago this December. In those thirty-seven years my wife has lived with five different men, and they have all been me. Every seven years your body changes, your personality goes through changes. She says it is more fun that way. But what's made her live with these five me's? She's a promise keeper. She also has a sense of humor, like the gal who said, "I don't want a perfect husband, just one who has faults I like." That helps. But I'm glad she's been a promise keeper.

The psalmist said, "The man who has a quiver full of children is the most happy fellow." Do you think he had teenagers when he wrote that? What makes a father tell himself, "I wish my daughter would pack up and leave home. She's driving us crazy." Then he remembers a promise he made when she was baptized or dedicated, and he sticks with her in hurting love. He's a promise keeper.

Let me read a few sentences of a letter I just got from Montreal. I was there a few years ago and one of the members of our committee died of a heart attack just before I got there. His son, who is now eighteen, wrote me a letter. I got it last week. He had just reread the book, *Sandy*, about our son who died. He said, "It helped me to think through what I'd gone through again. The one thing that struck me as I read last night is where you said, 'Because of Sandy's accomplishment and testimony and impact, our's was a clean grief.' There is nothing I thank the Lord for more than the fact that my Dad lived for God, and as a result I can have a "clean" grief. I need never worry about skeletons to hide. There are none." I wonder how many of our children could write that? In this age of throw-away relationships, are we going to be the kind of promise keepers who go beyond convenience and are ready to say to my family, "I promise you fidelity"?

LOYALTY

A third key word for promise keepers is *loyalty*. Am I a promise keeper in my friendships? How many of us are real friends? How many of us have real friends? Old buddies, acquaintances, and associates, yes—like-minded, like-income people who vote like us and have the same golf handicap and are safe until the bottom falls out.

These definitions of a friend are among my favorites: "A friend never gets in your way unless you are falling." From the Bible: "There is a friend that sticks closer than a brother." I like this one: "A friend is someone who when you make a fool of yourself doesn't think you've done a permanent job." Robert Coles, the Harvard psychiatrist, was in my hometown of Charlotte recently. He said, "The best practice of psychotherapy is two friends getting to know one another and sharing with one another."

I like that great demonstration of friendship in the Bible between Jonathan and David. Jonathan was supposed to be king. His father was king and he was supposed to be next. But David came in and became king. Instead of being consumed with jealousy, "Jonathan loved David as he loved his own soul." Even when his father turned viciously on David, Jonathan stuck with him at the risk of his own life.

How many of us have and are friends like that? Friends who walk in when the whole world walks out. Promise keepers who say to their friends, "I promise you loyalty."

PROMISE KEEPING IS NOT ALWAYS EASY

Sometimes we make promises we shouldn't. Sometimes we have to break one promise to keep another. Sometimes there are dilemmas. Let's 'fess up. Every one of us is a promise breaker. We haven't all been promise keepers all the way. That's why perhaps our greatest need if we want to be promise keepers is to start or restart our relationship with the ultimate promise keeper, the God who says, "I'll forgive you if you turn back to Me. I will be with you if you will trust in Me."

I talked a few days ago with Charles Colson who founded Prison Fellowship Ministries after prison for his part in Watergate. Colson had just been down to Brazil where Prison Fellowship runs a prison. They don't just have volunteers in the prison; they run the prison and staff it with Prison Fellowship volunteers.

The inmates run the security. It's tough but they run it; they have Bible studies and rehabilitation programs. The return rate to the prison is less than 5 percent. Often, at other prisons, it's 70-90 percent.

When Colson went to visit, he said as he always does, "Do you have a solitary confinement cell?"

"Yes."

"Can I see it?"

"Do you want to?"

"Yes."

So they took him downstairs and he walked through this basement, past where the former junta's torture chambers were located, down to the end of the corridor where they stopped at a big door.

The guide said to him, "You sure you want to go in?"

"Sure I want to go in," Colson replied.

So he opened this big, heavy door, turned the handle, and began to pull it open, stopped again, and repeated the question, "Mr. Colson, are you sure you want to go *in* there?"

Colson said, "Of course, I always go in to visit whoever's in solitary."

So they pulled the door open, and Chuck Colson told me, "I walked inside that cell and there was a table with two candles and some flowers and a picture of Jesus Christ on the Cross." The inmate guide said, "That's the Guy who is doing time for us."

That's the guy who is doing time for us. What brought Christ to that cross? It wasn't just Roman soldiers, but a promise—that God would send a Savior. What held Him on that cross? Not just nails, but a promise that He would lay down His life for us. What brought Him back to life? A promise, because God said, "I will not let sin and evil and death overcome." What brings Him into our lives and keeps Him there? A promise: "I stand at the door and knock. If you open that door, I will come in and I will walk your daily path with you."

God is a promise keeper, a God who says, "I am He who will be with you."

God Is a Promise Keeper

Gary Oliver

I grew up in Southern California and my favorite activity was swimming. There is only one time that I had to be rescued. When I was in ninth grade I went with some older friends to Tamarack State Beach near Oceanside, California for a day of body-surfing. The waves were great that day. I decided to swim a little farther from shore in hopes of catching some larger waves.

I was so intent on catching the waves I didn't notice that the waves were beginning to break in a pattern that can produce rip tides. As I was swimming farther out, I dove underneath a wave that was breaking right in front of me. Rather than immediately coming back up to the surface I felt tremendous pressure pushing my body down and pulling me out to sea. I had no idea what was happening. My feet touched the bottom. I tried to push myself up but couldn't. I was almost out of air and I panicked. I also prayed.

I forget what I said to God but obviously He heard me. Suddenly I found myself on the surface of the water. I was exhausted and afraid it would happen again. I heard a voice shouting to me. I turned towards the voice to see a lifeguard throwing a life preserver towards me. It had a rope attached to it. I grabbed the life preserver and hung on for dear life. With the rope in one hand the lifeguard pulled me in.

When I made it to shore I was a bit embarrassed but most of all I was grateful. The lifeguard said he had been watching me. He could see there was a rip tide condition and knew I wasn't aware of it. Before I had gone under he was already swimming towards me to warn me and if necessary rescue me.

Over the years I've realized that living the Christian life is a lot like the experience I had that day. Even though I wasn't aware of it, the lifeguard had his eyes on me and knew I was moving into dangerous water. He was in the water before I needed him—just in case.

God is our lifeguard. In Psalm 139:1-6 we are told that God is aware of every aspect of our lives. He is "intimately acquainted" with all our ways. In Psalm 121 we find that He never sleeps, and He never slumbers. He is on guard twenty-four hours a day.

As a young boy I remember attending a service at the Church of the Open Door in downtown Los Angeles and hearing Ethel Waters sing "His Eye Is on the Sparrow." Twenty-five years later the memory of her rendition of that classic hymn still stirs my spirit. The last phrase of the song is, "His eye is on the sparrow, and I know he watches me." It is taken from Matthew 6:26 and 10:29-31 and is another illustration of His concern for us.

God's promises are like life preservers. They keep the soul from sinking in the sea of discouragement. What exactly is a promise? Webster defines a promise as "(1) One's pledge to another to do or not to do something specified, a declaration which gives to the person to whom it is made a right to expect or to claim the performance or forbearance of a specified action."

When your perspective becomes distorted and your problems begin to consume your entire field of vision, you need a perspective preserver. When it feels like God has deserted you and you begin to get discouraged, you will find that God's promises will always pull you out and bring you back to safety.

KEY PROMISES

Several years ago I made a list of some key promises and put them on 3x5 cards. The verses include:

Psalm 37:1-7, 40:1-3;
Matthew 6:33;
Romans 8:28-29, 31, 37-39;

1 Corinthians 10:3-5;
Philippians 1:6, 2:13, 4:4-8, 13, 19.

Whenever I feel the rip tide of life pulling me under, I grab the cards, read them, and thank God for each one of them. For over twenty years it has worked for me. I know it has worked for thousands of others. I know it will work for you.

The story has been told of a believer, Frederick Nolan, who was fleeing from his enemies during a time of persecution in North Africa. Pursued by them over hill and valley with no place to hide, he fell exhausted into a wayside cave, expecting his enemies to find him soon.

Awaiting his death, he saw a spider weaving a web. Within minutes, the little bug had woven a beautiful web across the mouth of the cave. The pursuers arrived and wondered if Nolan was hiding there, but on seeing the unbroken and untangled piece of art, thought it impossible for him to have entered the cave without dismantling the web. And so they went on. Having escaped, Nolan burst out and exclaimed: "Where God is, a spider's web is like a wall. Where God is not, a wall is like a spider's web."

You will not always feel God's presence. There will be times when what is going on around you makes no sense at all. You may feel like you are drowning in discouragement. You may feel helpless and hopeless with no visible way of escape.

One of our family's favorite movies is *Mary Poppins*. In one scene the two children, Jane and Michael Banks, jumped into bed after their first day with the amazing Mary Poppins. Jane asked, "Mary Poppins, you won't ever leave us, will you?" Michael, full of excitement, looked at his new nanny and added, "Will you stay if we promise to be good?" Mary looked at the two and as she tucked them in she replied, "Look, that's a pie-crust promise. Easily made, easily broken."

God's promises to us weren't easily made and they have never been broken. God makes a promise, faith believes it, hope anticipates it, and patience quietly awaits it. Claim it. Believe it. Anticipate it. Wait for it.

2

The Promises You Make to God

Gary Smalley and John Trent

The way to ensure growth as a promise keeper is to be lovingly planted and nurtured. The Bible tells us that the only way to be lovingly planted and nurtured is to begin your promise keeper quest with God:

> Blessed is the man who does not walk
>   in the counsel of the wicked
> or stand in the way of sinners
> or sit in the seat of mockers.
> But his delight is in the law of the LORD,
>   and on his law he meditates
>   day and night.
> He is like a tree planted by streams of water,
>   which yields its fruit in season. . .
> Whatever he does prospers. (Psalm 1:1-3)

The articles in this section focus on this beginning, the basics needed to effectively live as a man of integrity.

Promises to God

William Gaultiere

Have you made promises to God? These may sound familiar: "I'll start reading my Bible every day. I'm going to get more involved at church. I'll pray for that person. I'm going to work harder at being the head of my home. I'll be more considerate of my wife. I'll spend more time with my kids. I'm going to be a better witness for Christ to my colleagues. I won't lose my temper again."

We've all made commitments like these to God time and time again. Often, promises to God come close on the heels of guilt. Perhaps you don't feel like you measure up so you promise to try harder, do more, do better . . . only to fall short again and lament to yourself, "I'll never be the Christian man I should be."

Or perhaps you feel like you do measure up. Have you climbed to the top of the mountain? Have you done what you should, fulfilled your commitments, pleased the people you care about? Have you reached the point of saying, "I've done it! God must be pleased with me now." Or is this just a secret hope. What will you do next—find another mountain to climb "for God"?

Or maybe you avoid the pitfalls of guilt and pride by not making promises to God. Perhaps you don't consider God in your decisions, daily schedules, relationships, thought life, or future aspirations. You probably feel your prayers bounce off the ceiling anyway. Bible reading seems dull to you. Church seems irrelevant. Your spiritual life is empty. You feel like you're just going through the motions. "So why should I even try?" you wonder.

The chances are, if you struggle with guilt, pride, or apathy in your spiritual life, you probably have a distorted image of God.

How do you experience your heavenly Father? What do you feel in your heart when you're alone with God? Maybe you feel some of the things you felt as a child when you were with your dad: pressure to measure up to his expectations, guilt for disappointing him, afraid he'll get mad at you, hesitant to express yourself for fear you'll be judged, sad because he doesn't really know you, anxious because you don't have his help and you know you're on your own in this world.

What is our heavenly Father really like?

Jesus gave us a picture of Him in the story known as the Parable of the Prodigal Son (Luke 15:11-32). One day the prodigal insults his father by saying, "Dad, give me the money due me when you die." Then he goes off to a faraway city where he lives a lavish and sinful lifestyle. There is a famine and the money runs through his fingers fast. Soon he is so hungry and desperate that he disgraces his Jewish identity by hiring himself out to feed pigs! Finally, he comes to his senses and returns home to his father.

How will his father receive him? How would your father receive you?

The prodigal's father misses his son so much that each day he goes out to his fields and looks to see if his son is coming. One day he sees his son walking toward him in the distance and he runs out to greet him! The son's face is hung in shame, his clothes are dirty and tattered, and he smells like the pigsty he came from, yet his father wraps his arms around him, hugs him close to his heart, and kisses him on the cheek! The father gives his son his best robe to wear. He gives him his signet ring so that he has power of attorney and a second chance with the remainder of the family estate. He puts sandals on his son's feet to welcome him back into his home as his child. He even throws a party for him!

We men who struggle with guilt, pride, or apathy are prodigal sons. The father is God. We need to experience the same kind of fatherly love and forgiveness in order to feel better about ourselves as men. When we do, we'll want to commit ourselves to love God and to share His love with others.

Promise to God, to yourself, and to another man that you'll open your heart to your heavenly Father's love for you.

A Man's Fixed Reference

Roger Palms

One Saturday in Houston, Texas, I toured the National Aeronautics and Space Administration (NASA). It was the same week that the second space shuttle, *Columbia*, was launched. I left the main tourist attractions and, escorted by a project engineer, climbed into the simulator, the practice unit of *Columbia*. It was an exact duplicate of the one that went into space.

As I sat in the commander's seat, I tried to imagine what it must be like to be in space. But even as I pretended, I knew that in reality I was on the ground. I will probably never get off the ground in a spacecraft. I can only guess what it might be like in space. I am earthbound; that is my reference point.

But others know what it is like not to have Earth as a reference point. Once in space astronauts think about a particular focus. They have to be strapped in someplace, or they float. They wear suction cups on their feet to enable them to stand. These suction cups release with a twist of the foot, then hold firm again with the proper placement. Astronauts need to be attached somewhere in order to work. If they aren't, they can't even push a switch on a computer, for in trying they push themselves backward. That's a problem with weightlessness.

And when they sleep, it doesn't matter whether they sleep on the "top" of the bunk or on the opposite side of it, the "bottom" of the bunk, or even sleep standing up. There is no "top" or "bottom," no "up" or "down" in space. They shut their eyes and their inner reference tells them that they are lying down. Since there is no weight, it doesn't matter which way they are facing when they sleep—up, down, or sideways. Sleep comes because their minds decide for them which way is up and which way is down.

We are in a weightless world too. There are no fixed reference points, no "up" or "down," no right way or wrong way. The only reference we have is in the mind of each person—we decide our reference point. We decide to what we will be tied; we determine each step we take. Without a reference point we aren't able to function. We can't accomplish anything.

In a society without fixed points we have to decide to make our own or we will be adrift, and every action will have a counter thrust to it.

Men have to be committed. Only those who determine that they will be, who have a reference point, will ever touch the world in a meaningful way. The Christian, with reference to the Rock and obedience to the high calling of God in Christ Jesus, has a reason for commitment.

Astronauts train their minds and fix a reference point; it is the only way they can live in their weightless environment. Christians do that too, all the time, in this "weightless" environment in which we live. For there are no fixed social values for us anymore, and if we function like the rest of society we will drift too. With no fixed position, no matter what we do, no matter what we try to push against, we will be useless.

In our daily existence only obedience to the guidance that God gives will keep us going; only commitment to Him will keep us from floating. We will walk only when we clamp down on Him—He alone is firm; He is unchanging. We stand or move in what is fixed—God—and we know that if we move from that point of reference we will start to drift again.

God is our focus; and because He is, we can act.

Doing What Our Heavenly Father Says

Luis Palau

More than ninety people conducted an all-night search several winters ago for Dominic DeCarlo, an eight-year-old boy lost on a snowy mountain slope. Dominic, who had been on a skiing trip with his father, apparently had ridden on a new lift and skied off the run without realizing it.

As each hour passed, the search party and the boy's family became more and more concerned for his safety and survival. By dawn they had found no trace of the young boy. Two helicopter crews joined the search and within fifteen minutes had spotted ski tracks. A ground team followed the tracks, which changed to small footprints. The footprints led to a tree, where they found the boy at last.

"He's in super shape!" Sergeant Terry Silbaugh, area search-and-rescue coordinator, announced to the anxious family and to the press. "In fact, he's in better shape than we are right now!" A hospital spokeswoman said the boy was in fine condition and wasn't even admitted.

Silbaugh explained why the boy did so well despite spending a night in the freezing elements: His father had enough forethought to tell the boy what to do if he became lost, and his son had enough trust to do exactly what his father said.

Dominic protected himself from possible frostbite and hypothermia by snuggling up to a tree and covering himself with branches. As a young child, he never would have thought of doing this on his own. He was simply obeying his wise and loving father.

Dominic reminds me of what we should do as men who are children of a loving and infinitely wise heavenly Father. We are not to walk according to the course of this world, which is passing away. Instead, we are to walk in obedience to the Lord's commands. After all, He knows what is best for us. That's one of the reasons I believe the Bible is so relevant for us today.

The apostle Peter tells us, "As obedient children, do not conform to the evil desires you had when you lived in ignorance. But just as he who called you is holy, so be holy in all you do; for it is written: 'Be holy, because I am holy'" (1 Peter 1:14-16).

In Christ, we enjoy a holy standing before God. In 2 Corinthians 5:21 we discover that "God made him who had no sin to be sin for us, so that in him we might become the righteousness of God." But our actual state here on earth is sometimes a different story.

Because our Father is holy, and because in Christ we have a holy standing, we are exhorted in Scripture to be holy in all that we do. Every time we sin, we are forgetting who we are and why we are alive. We are forgetting what is truly best for us. Yes, we can find forgiveness from the Father when we sin (1 John 2:1-2), but sin is not to be the trademark of our lives.

In a world full of deceptive detours and confusing paths, let's trust our heavenly Father and do exactly what He has said.

Whose Man?

John Yates

There are at least three types of men—a "ladies' man," a "man's man," and "God's man." At some point a man needs to decide what sort of man he aims to be.

A "ladies' man" seeks the admiration and attention of women. He is always conscious of how he is coming across to the opposite sex. He dresses for this and pursues feminine companionship consistently. His ultimate goal is sexual fulfillment. Eros, deep down, drives him towards women. Though most often single, marriage does not necessarily convert a ladies' man into a family man. Many families are broken apart because the father could not give up being a ladies' man.

Aiming at being a "man's man" is, I think, a nobler goal than that of being a ladies' man. The man's man desires the respect of other men. He wants to be listened to and admired by his male peers, to be highly esteemed, to succeed in the eyes of other men. The man's man works hard at his work and hard at his play. Just as most men sometimes feel insecure in regard to the opposite sex, so we also are not totally secure with other men. But we want to be, so we strive for acceptance and respect through our work, our reputation, our manner with others.

In the best sense of the phrase, a man's man is one who has grown to the place of feeling secure in himself. He is firm without being pushy. He is genuine and real without being an exhibitionist. He is compassionate but not sentimental; honest, true to his word; he is humble but willing to take on responsibility. A man's man takes responsibility for his failures, without making excuses.

He is an achiever, committed to excellence, confident but not reckless. He is personable but not overly familiar. He is the sort of man we want as our friend, the sort we want to be.

A man's man believes that character is more important than "success." He does not follow when the crowd goes in an opposite direction. He is wise enough not to accept rumors, not to make snap judgments, not to judge by appearances alone. He knows his mind, pursues his own goals, but is willing to submit his one wants for the greater good of the whole.

To be esteemed a man's man is a genuine honor. But this, in the long run, is still not a sufficient goal for a man to pursue, if he wants to become all he can become. For if it is true that there is a God; if God is personal and may be known; if God cares for us individually; if He bestows particular gifts upon men and designs our individual callings and destinies; if God offers us His friendship, His guidance, and strength; and if we are created by Him in His image, then it is not enough just to be a man's man, for even the man's man remains incomplete unless he knows God. Our highest and noblest goal is to be God's man.

What does it mean to be God's man? It means being a man's man but more. To be God's man means to be the friend of God and the servant of God, who wants, above all, the will of God. God's man knows and trusts that God's way is the best way, and therefore commits himself daily to discerning, as best he can, the will of God in all situations. He sees his life, his abilities, his possessions, his family as gifts entrusted to him by God. All he has belongs to God. Living God's way matters more than anything else. As he matures, he becomes aware of his weaknesses, and when he fails God or others, he acknowledges it with sorrow and humility. He is teachable and willing to learn from anyone and any situation. He knows his own need for the Savior and therefore does not condemn or give up on others who demonstrate their own foolishness or fallenness. He is patient, persistent, and consistent in his commitment to live out the principles of Jesus. When he falls short of God's best, he doesn't condemn himself but weeps within himself that he has yet to become all God wants him to be.

God's man is no carbon copy of another. He is an original who refuses to let others do his thinking for him, but seeks always to bring the mind-set of Christ and the perspective of God to whatever decisions, plans, or relationships confront him. He is God's man. Whose man are you?

3

The Promises You Make to Yourself

Gary Smalley and John Trent

I f you could somehow freeze-frame biblical manhood or in some way boil it down into its component parts, you would see five elements that are always present. These key ingredients can be learned by a woman, but they set a man apart as a man. All of them are powerful reflections of the kind of man Jesus Christ was, and of what we need to be as well.

As you read the next three chapters, we'll be examining these five marks of masculinity in the contexts where they apply the most. However, keep in mind that they come as a package and define your masculinity in *any* context, not just with yourself, your wife, or your family. We've chosen to discuss them in these contexts for the purposes of this book, but we want you to keep in mind their ever-present nature in all of us as men.

Our goal in sharing these is, again, to help us all develop into men who honor God and demonstrate the convictions, integrity, and actions of Christlike men—men who can keep a promise.

As you read through this list, ask yourself how your father reflected these traits . . . and how well you model them for your own children.

ASSERTIVENESS

When you look at the person of Christ, you're looking at assertiveness. He healed the lame on the Sabbath day, even when the religious leaders stood in His face and dared Him to do so. He cast money-changers from the temple and tossed verbal bombshells at the Pharisees that exploded the wall of hypocrisy surrounding them. He chased away demons and faced up to the prince of darkness. In all these situations He relied on the healthy assertion of His power.

One mark of a man is the natural assertiveness that flows through his blood. Even toddlers reflect it.

Instead of accepting the answer of ivory-tower radicals who expound theories of androgyny and blur the distinction between the sexes, spend some time talking to the mother of a boy and a girl. Their behavior patterns from the earliest ages show marked differences in natural aggression.

My (John's) oldest brother, Joe, and his wife, Marnel, have two wonderful children—a girl and a boy. Mindy came along nearly four weeks premature, but with a fully developed peacefulness and warmth that has stayed with her for twelve years.

With Mindy, Joe and Marnel never bothered to put away the decorative glass apple on the coffee table. One firm "no" the first time she picked up the crystal object and she obediently put it down and went on to other more acceptable playthings.

Then Joseph came along. All boy, and all excited at his new-found toddling skills, he headed for the coffee table and saw the pretty, crystal apple.

"No, no," said Marnel, in her sweet, calm voice. "Put it down."

"*Slam, slam, slam, slam!*" Joseph did put it down, smashing it down on the table as hard as he could to see if it would break (or at least to see how much noise it could make!).

Within a week, everything breakable in the house had been evacuated from harm's way to avoid the might of this two-foot warrior of Diaper Storm!

It is in our deepest nature as men to push forward, to step out, to take charge, to fight for higher ground. The Shulammite woman saw this trait in Solomon and admired it as she said of his assertiveness, "Draw me after you, and let us run together."

But while healthy assertiveness is an admirable trait, many men grow up taking two different directions that curve away from healthy assertiveness—and Christlikeness.

Getting Paid for Doing Nothing

One group of men who follow the low road could be on the cover of the best-selling book *Passive Men and Wild Women*.

Many secular and Christian counselors have observed and commented on the problem of motivating a passive husband. Actually, while having a problem with motivation himself, he has no problem motivating his desperate wife to be assertive!

The subtle snare that pulls at an unmotivated man is the faulty notion that there is a payoff to inactivity! The more a man hides from legitimate responsibilities . . . like taking an active role in family decisions, being the spiritual leader of the home, getting involved in the lives of the children, even putting bread on the table . . . the more the pressure builds up inside the home. And the reward for too many men is that if they just sit still long enough (usually just like Dad did), then the pressure will finally catapult their wife into a frenzy of activity.

Soon, instead of a marriage team, there's only one player on the field, and she's exhausted. There may be two people in the backfield, but only one carries the ball until she's often ready to give up the game and quit the team. The more passive he gets, the wilder she becomes, and the worse the model they project for the children who are watching them.

Laziness is a learned activity, and healthy assertiveness can be learned as well. "Go to the ant, you sluggard, and learn," said Solomon, the wisest man who lived. There are no goldbrickers on an ant pile, and no truly masculine men who don't carry their load with their family and work responsibilities.

If you're missing this first mark of masculinity, then it's time to take a close look at your past and fill in the hole. But make sure that you don't fill it by going to the opposite extreme when it comes to being assertive. We can have Christlike assertiveness without being domineering.

Angry All the Time

If one aspect of assertiveness abuse is seen in those who passively refuse to take action, another is found with the man who thinks assertiveness equals anger. For many men, the ability to be assertive is like a light switch; either they're in the "off" position, lying on the couch; or they're in the "on" position, pointing an angry index finger or shouting dramatically that they're in control.

But assertiveness doesn't have to be all "on" or all "off." One of the most assertive men I've (John) ever known was someone who never raised his voice to be assertive, he didn't have to. My wrestling coach in high school was a combat veteran of the Korean War and a former collegiate all-American. While the other coaches I had over the years would rant and rave at you for making a mistake, Coach Curtis would do something much more intimidating. If you broke one of his cardinal rules, he would calmly walk over, stand right in front of you, his eyes locked inches from yours, and quietly—yet powerfully—issue correction or instructions. He never shouted. But there was thunder in Coach Curtis' quiet voice, and you listened when he spoke to you.

Jesus' inner assertiveness didn't make Him less attractive as a man; it added to His ability to lead others. But His strength was always tempered in love, not testing or tyrannical. Unfortunately, there have been many who have abused this aspect of power and masculinity, and with unhealthy effects.

Recently, a group of women at Brigham Young University issued a proclamation that "All men should be forced to stay indoors on Thursday nights." Generating national coverage, their spokeswoman explained, "I want one night of the week when I'm not afraid to walk through the campus."

For this woman, having men locked away one night a week would be the solution (even though there had been only one incident of a woman being assaulted on campus, and that was at 9:00 a.m.). One would hope that she would never leave the city of Provo and journey to the streets of New York!

Whatever her motives, what she and her feminist friends are reacting to is a natural—and if abused—scary side of a man: his assertiveness. However, chaining a lion one night a week won't make him a lap cat.

Men are powerful. But the answer to harnessing that power isn't to lock it away as an undesirable trait, but link it with a second aspect of biblical manhood.

SELF-CONTROL

You're a corrupt Roman governor who can sense deep inside that the black clouds of judgment are just over the horizon. But for now, the storm is out of view. And perhaps to avert its coming fury, you're looking for some way to ease the guilt, to relieve the burden you've created by your own acts, particularly over what you did to your brother.

At night, in the covering of darkness, having his beautiful widow as your wife seems like a dream. But every morning, pieces of the nightmare still creep back. For after all, it was your order that had your brother murdered so you could marry his wife.

Perhaps a talk with the prisoner Paul, the follower of Jesus, would help. The gods' favor you're used to finding can be bought and sold at the temple. Perhaps with his God, there's a price you could pay that would provide a celestial coverup to the act you've committed.

But all your talk does is elevate your guilt to anxiety!

You're a ruler who holds the power of life or death over that prisoner, but it's the captive who strikes fear in your heart. Not by his presence, which was unassuming, almost contemptible, but by his words. Those three things he talked about brought so much fear, it was like a noose tightening around your neck, until you finally told him to go away, for now.

Those three things held the ring of truth. They must hold the key to getting the burden off your back . . . but the cost. What Paul shared with Felix that acted like shock therapy to his system are three things that can cause us to freeze-up inside as well. In Acts 24, we see the story of Paul and Felix and a trio of confrontative truths.

Two of the issues Paul talked about are great theological truths. We'd expect both of them to appear on almost any preacher's short list of convicting sermons. His twin themes of "righteousness" and "the judgment to come" set forth the standard we all miss—and the price for missing it.

But sandwiched between these two expected topics is an unexpected one. Something more personal than theological. Something that moves from preaching to meddling, from arm's length to eye to eye. And something we think Felix found every bit as convicting as the other two—or maybe more so.

On the outside, Felix had things under control. He was a ruler, after all—with the full weight of Rome behind his seal. But on the inside he lacked something whose obvious absence led to so much of his guilt and fear and lack of self-control.

As we look at the various marks of masculinity, this one is unmistakable. There is nothing more powerful in a man than a deep, inner sense of self-control.

Self-control is the strength to keep your tongue still when everyone else at work is ripping the boss to shreds behind his back. It's the resolve to turn past the "late night" movie selection in the hotel room, even when you're all alone. It's the courage to count to ten, and then to ten again, instead of ripping into your spouse or teenager when she irritates you.

In Proverbs, we read that "He who is slow to anger is better than the mighty, and he who rules his spirit, than he who captures a city." Ruling our spirit. Keeping tabs on our temper. Slowing down our responses so that we act in a responsible way, instead of simply reacting in a selfish way. These are earmarks of self-control—and true masculinity. And something else.

The degree of self-control you have in your life is in direct proportion to the degree of acceptance you have for yourself. Put another way, if you don't value yourself, you won't "pull in the reins" on actions and attitudes that will affect you for the worse.

In biblical Greek, one word picture behind the word *self-control* is the idea of pulling in the reins on a horse—or a habit. It's the failure to "pull in the reins" that lies at the heart of any addiction. And what keeps a person's hands away from the reins too often is a deep inner sense of powerlessness and rejection—no matter how "together" we look on the outside.

Our friend Wade is a classic example of this all-too-common cycle. The son of a TV celebrity, Wade grew up watching his father live out one image on the screen, and a very different one at home. Dad was strong and in control in each continuing episode, yet totally controlled by the bottle when he stepped away from the cameras.

Wade grew up resenting his father, and in a deeper way, disliking himself for being like him. He became a master at keeping up the outer image, just like Dad. And deep inside, he was setting himself up for failure.

A successful life is built from the inside out. But Wade tried to reverse the process. By never dealing with the hole in his heart, he ignored a deep inner dislike for himself. He perfected an outer image as a Christian leader, making whatever sacrifices it took to move up the ladder of fame and respect. But in his personal life, he failed to "pull in the reins" on his growing habit of "social drinking."

It wasn't until he lost both his ministry and his family that he finally had to confront his problems. He told us, "I used to blame everything on my father. But then I saw that the enemy was actually me. People would praise me for something I'd accomplish, but I'd never really believe it. I had a beautiful wife and outstanding ministry, but I hated myself. And my closet drinking was just one more way to prove to myself that I really wasn't valuable, no matter what anyone else said. For somebody who set out to 'never be like my dad,' I did a great job of becoming just like him."

To what degree are you exhibiting self-control over your emotions, appetites, and actions? Whether you're hooked on cable TV channels, sexual temptation, out-of-control spending, or substance abuse—if you're caught up in the first steps of any addiction or twenty miles down the road, there's a hole in your heart, an inner hurt, and dislike of self that can make you worthy of failure, but not success.

To bring this point down to basics, let's take a look at a commonplace happening in a common work setting. Jim is a new employee, working on the shipping docks because it's the only job available. He's hardworking, doesn't abuse coffee breaks, and seems very overqualified to turn big piles into little piles.

What's the natural thing to do with Jim after a few months of exemplary service have gone by? Promote him, of course!

He's obviously capable of handling more responsibility, and even overseeing the work of others. But what the employer misses is that he has a hole in his heart.

On a "1" to "10" scale, let's say Jim's innermost sense of self-worth is about a "2." That came from an abusive father, an overcontrolling mother, failed potential, and consistently ruined promising relationships with the "right" girl.

With two years of college behind him and a truckload of untapped talent, Jim looks like what he should become, a leader! And he even realizes that working as the lowest man on the shipping dock is a "2" of a job. But the problem is, it's so comfortable.

What happens next is what's happened before. He gets called into the boss's office and given a major promotion. Now instead of a "2" he's placed in a position where he needs to be assertive and have self-control. It's an "8" of a job, with the pay and privileges to go with it. So what happens next?

Does he live up to the challenge and make his mark on the company? Or does he self-destruct and again carry the mark of lost potential along with his severance check?

You make the call. But if you said he'd self-destruct, you'd be right more than 90 percent of the time. Why? Because a person who views himself as a "2" in either business or personal relationships will actually begin to provoke others to treat him that way! And one of the easiest ways to seize failure from the jaws of success is to suddenly lose self-control.

You sleep through your alarm again and miss the supervisor's meeting for the second time this week. You "forget" to mark down a three-hour lunch break on your timecard, but an audit by your superior helps jog your memory. Your dress becomes sloppier, your drive runs out of gas, and your work totals count for less.

You're a casualty of a self-inflicted wound from childhood that has never healed. Habits of failure can be formed in a difficult past. But they can also be broken. We can become more healthily assertive and more in control of our lives. It is possible to gain the self-control we need to have successful relationships. But not without first confronting ourselves. And not without filling the holes in our hearts.

Making Promises to Yourself

Make a promise to yourself as you seek to become a promise keeper to God and others. Promise yourself to submit your assertiveness to God, that He may use it in ways that are appropriate to His purposes—ways that will honor Him.

Similarly, promise yourself that you'll seek to develop self-control. It's another key to developing masculine habits that reflect a heart being healed by Christ.

Masculinity

Larry Crabb

A man is "manly" when he moves through life with purposeful and confident involvement, when he follows a direction that he values for reasons that are bigger than himself. If that direction reflects the purposes of God, then his style of relating will not be self-consumed, driven, or pushy; it will rather reflect a growing sensitivity to others and an unhurried involvement with them that can be neither manipulated nor stopped. Indications that he is pulling appreciation or applause or confirmation from others to feed either an oversized or a starving ego will lessen the enjoyable impact of his masculinity on both himself and others.

When a man's purposes are godly, that is, when he is ambitious for God's glory and concerned with other-centered relating, he will experience a stability that anchors him through emotional ups and downs (which he will therefore be unafraid to experience) and a noble desire for tender, caring, intimate involvement with people, primarily his wife. In this involvement his wife will feel secure, conscious that she is more enjoyed and valued than his greatest achievements.

Masculinity is not so much a matter of what a man does, but that he does it and that he does it for certain reasons. Little things, for example, like rubbing your wife's neck when it is sore, will be felt as "masculine" even though another man or a woman could provide the same service for your wife, and perhaps more competently. It is the demonstrated and eager sensitivity to another's need that feels masculine to both partners when a husband rubs his wife's sore neck.

A masculine man knows, with a sense of gratitude rather than pride, that there will be impact for good as he moves into his world, and that what he gives is most worthy of respect when it touches the longings of his wife's heart. Masculinity disposes a man to move decisively and compassionately into his world and toward family and friends with a joyful confidence that he can promote good purposes.

When the substance within him that defines his male identity is moving with other-centered energy, a man feels a completion and wholeness that make selfish achievement and immoral pleasures less appealing. Nothing brings a man quite the same level of masculine pleasure as touching his wife in a way that brings her joy and confidence as a woman and that frees her to enjoy all that she is and can become.

Masculinity, I suggest, might therefore be thought of as *the satisfying awareness of the substance God has placed within a man's being that can make an enduring contribution to God's purposes in this world, and will be deeply valued by others . . . as a reliable source of wise, sensitive, compassionate, and decisive involvement.*

Grace and Guilt

Andrew T. LePeau

W
hat drives us to prayer? What motivates us to evangelize? What compels us to help the needy? If you are like
me, the surprising answer is often guilt.

I ought to get up at four every morning to pray, I tell myself,
instead of waiting till right before bed. I ought to memorize the
book of Leviticus instead of reciting John 3:16. I ought to fast and
pray twice a week instead of merely skipping breakfast because I
overslept.

I ought to teach junior high Sunday school and take that head
usher job and volunteer at the recycling center and take an hour a
day with each of my children and remodel the kitchen. I may have
even tried valiantly to meet one or two of these goals. But did I
succeed? No. I did not. And as a result I label myself a chronic
spiritual failure.

But there is good news. That good news is the grace of God.
The apostle Paul said, "It is for freedom that Christ has set us free"
(Galatians 5:1, NIV). Christ reconciled us to God and freed us from
sin so we can live in freedom. We are no longer judged by legalis-
tic expectations that other Christians might impose on us. The
good news is that now God loves us completely regardless of what
we do or don't do.

Too often I imagine that my good deeds somehow make me
more acceptable to God than I am in Christ alone. But that is not
true. Because of Christ and His death, God finds great pleasure in
me just the way I am.

Why do we too often find prayer a drudgery, church a chore,

evangelism distasteful, and giving joyless? Despite the many times we may have heard that we are saved by grace through faith alone, we just don't act like it. We became Christians by grace, but we still think we have to earn God's love. This is a lie. Nothing is required. We are free. This is the new, glorious, liberated state Christ intended for us when He set us free from sin.

You may be asking along with opponents of Paul, "Shall we go on sinning so that grace may increase?" And with Paul I answer, "By no means!" (Romans 6:1-2, NIV). Because God considers me dead to the law, He won't judge me by it. My response to this is not to want to start sinning—it is amazed love and gratitude! I seek to please God not because I have to, but because I want to.

In contrast to grace, guilt is actually a very poor motivator. It bears little fruit and wears off too quickly. Off and on over the years I have, for example, fallen into thinking that I had to have a quiet time because I knew I was supposed to. But when I did, the joy wore off, and I grew little as a result. At such times, of course, I struggle to have my daily quiet time even once a week.

But when I remember what life in Christ is all about, I have a very different experience. I don't feel guilty if I miss a day, but I don't want to miss. I know God loves me, and I look forward to being with Him.

It is easy to be misled by those who try to make us feel guilty because we are not doing enough. Some Christian leaders may make much of observing minor requirements of conduct and emphasize their own authority in such matters. The truth is, however, that we are free from petty rules and obligations. We have a higher calling and a higher motivation—the love of God.

Men of Gratitude

Harold L. Bussell

Seated around the dinner table for our traditional Appreciation Dinner, we told my eighty-two-year-old father all the
things we appreciated about him. This is a family tradition
that usually takes place prior to the departure of a guest in our
home. My father had just spent two months with us enjoying a
New England Christmas and renewing his spirits after my mother's
recent death. The next morning he left to return to California and
within ten days he passed from this life. I am thankful our last
words together were words of gratitude.

But gratitude doesn't come naturally, and I am thankful my wife
taught me to be a grateful man. Gratitude is not easy because when
we express gratitude, we acknowledge our need for others' expressions of love and care. We become vulnerable. In showing gratitude
we admit our need for another person's relationship, insight, or
help. By saying "thanks" we subtly admit our dependence on
another person. This is the opposite of serving self.

Ingratitude does come naturally. In the book of Romans, chapter 1, Paul says that the root of all rebellion is not a clinched fist
toward God, a drive to do one's own thing, but an attitude of
ingratitude. "For although they knew God, they neither glorified
him as God nor gave thanks. . . . Therefore God gave them over to
the sinful desires of their hearts" (Romans 1:21,24).

Isn't much of our stress in the family rooted in ingratitude?
We are ungrateful for our families by comparing them to others,
for our possessions by desiring more, and the saga continues.
Ungrateful people never get enough. They need more—more

things, more power, or more recognition.

Are you a grateful man? Grateful men lower their defenses toward God and others. Gratitude deepens relationships and builds a defense against Satan. Grateful men are enjoyable to be around. Gratitude opens doors to reconciliation and declares my need for God and others. Grateful men invite honesty and forgiveness to be a part of their lives. Genuine appreciation creates an environment for resisting temptation, resolving conflicts, and soothing hurts.

Americans pride themselves in being independent, but so does Satan. Our nation's history did not begin at the signing of the Declaration of Independence. Rather, it began one hundred fifty years earlier when the Pilgrims knelt in gratitude to declare their dependence on Almighty God to carry them through another year. Grateful men know the joy of thanking God and others. Gratitude is the greatest gift a man can give to his child, wife, friend, employer, employee, and God.

The Truth Will Set You Free

Bill Sanders

How well do you know yourself? Do you really understand why you do what you do, what makes you happy or sad, and why you may have a constant search for peace that isn't there? I'm not talking just about people who do not know Jesus Christ. I'm talking to Christian men . . . and I'm one of them.

I'm forty years old and considered successful. I have written eight books, traveled around the world, and shared the platform with some wonderful people such as President Ford, President Reagan, Chuck Swindoll, Frank Peretti, Zig Ziglar, and others. But it wasn't until this year, at the age of forty, that I realized how the truth can set you free.

Spiritually we all know that understanding the truth of God's love and His plan of salvation and forgiveness and mercy can set us free from the worry of ever going to hell. It can set us free from ever having to spend eternity anywhere but in Heaven.

The kind of freedom I'm talking about is emotional. Yes, I'm a Christian and have been walking with the Lord for thirteen years. He is my Lord, my Savior, and my best Friend. He has guided me through the good and the bad and the ugly. He has given me a wonderful home, the greatest marriage on the face of the earth, three of the most beautiful and wonderful children there have ever been, but I still had something missing. I didn't understand myself.

I am one of those people who always thought counseling was for people who were crazy. But when little things irritated me more than ever before and anger became a daily habit—enough was enough. For my kids' sake, I had to get help. I wanted to stop this and understand where it was coming from. If a man could have PMS, I had it and it could come up at any time, but especially when my kids got loud or something didn't go right.

What I found out in my counseling was that my childhood was less than perfect. I always pretended it was wonderful. The role that I played was the great pretender . . . the mascot . . . the successful kid. To hide the void where love and attention should have been, I pursued success. Over the years, since the age of sixteen, I have run my own business. Neighbors and friends used to say how responsible I was and how wonderful it was that I had my own business and was doing such a good job. I filled the void where love and a healthy self-worth should have been by doing things that got me recognition. My parents had their troubles and an unhealthy relationship with one another, leaving them with little time, energy, and effort to effectively and lovingly give us kids the nurturing we needed.

When I found that I was filling my void with success, it finally (for the first time in my life) all made sense. I *had* to write books, speak to kids by the thousands, answer each and every letter they wrote to me (nearly 3,000 a year in recent years), travel across the country, and then notify the newspapers so they would know about it, so I could feel good about Bill Sanders.

The truth will set you free. I am free now from having to do what I always thought I had to do in order for people to think I was a worthy person. I still write books and talk to thousands of kids because it is my desire and passion . . . and it is where God has placed me. I still travel across the world and look forward to my next trip to Russia to hand out Bibles, but for the first time in my life I don't need to write the books and be recognized in order to feel good about Bill Sanders. I do what I do because God has placed the desire in my heart . . . and not because I have to.

Do you have problems that are ruining your relationships? I strongly urge you to consider taking counseling. Big boys do cry, and crying is very healthy. In this day and age where "macho" is in, I challenge you to get the help that you need. If you had a painful childhood and it controls your life each and every day, get help! I promise you (I've seen it firsthand), the truth will set you free.

God Loves Losers, Too!

Ken Abraham

Our society places an enormous amount of pressure on us to succeed. Rarely do you see an athlete on television running toward the camera with two fingers pointed in the air as he shouts, "We're number two! We're number two!" No, being number one is what life is all about.

At least, that is what we are taught.

Unfortunately, Christians have the annoying habit of using worldly standards and superficial measuring sticks to determine levels of success and the value of a person. In one area after another, Christians are adopting the world's ideas of what it means to be a winner. Yet even more alarming, we have allowed these false, warped values to color, confound, and confuse what it means to be a success in our personal spiritual adventures.

Consequently, multitudes of modern men feel like abject failures in their spiritual lives. Why?

Because they don't love Jesus?

No.

Because they have not repented of their sins?

No.

Because the Lord has not forgiven them?

No.

Why, then?

Because, while desperately desiring to be successful in their spiritual lives, they have been sucked into the snare of measuring their progress by worldly standards. They insist upon comparing themselves to everybody else. They try to measure up on their own effort or merit. They are trying to be "good" under their own power. Frustration soon follows when these sincere believers realize they have failed . . . again.

The devil has defeated these Christians through one of his most devious devices: He has deceived them into pursuing a false path of personal perfectionism. They operate under their own power, comparing their success or lack of success with artificially imposed standards of perfection; they are on a perpetual treadmill, traveling the road to nowhere except fatigue, discouragement, and exhaustion.

It is important for us to recall the word that God gave to the prophet Zechariah: "'Not by might nor by power, but by my Spirit,' says the LORD of hosts" (Zechariah 4:6, NASB). God told His prophet that His temple would be built; His mighty work would get done, but it would not be because of sheer human effort. It would have a supernatural touch upon it.

That same touch is needed in your life if you are ever to overcome your spiritual impotence. Try as you might with your own strength, you will never perfectly please the Lord. The secret to true success is "Christ in you, the hope of glory" (Colossians 1:27, NASB).

Disorderly Conduct

Steve Farrar

Most guys I know don't worry too much about anorexia or bulimia. But they should. As you probably know, anorexia nervosa and bulimia are eating disorders that affect young women primarily. But most men I know do deal with one or the other on the spiritual level.

What is anorexia? It is extreme body emaciation caused by an emotional or psychological aversion to food and eating. Some young women afflicted with this disorder will allow their body weight to get down to half of what is normal. The tragedy is that some of these young women eventually starve themselves to death.

Spiritual anorexia is an aversion to feeding from the Word of God. It is impossible for a man to stand and fight in spiritual warfare if he is spiritually malnourished. This is why the enemy will do whatever is necessary to keep us from reading and meditating on the Scriptures. Jesus put it this way in His dialogue with Satan: "Man shall not live by bread alone, but on every word that proceeds out of the mouth of God."

If a man is not consistently taking in the Scriptures, then he will be weak and sickly and easily overcome by temptation. A man may believe in the Bible and even revere it, but if a man is not feeding from the Bible, he is easy prey for the enemy. That's why the enemy attempts to disrupt the appointments that we make to meet with the Lord and His Word.

I recently came across a tremendous tool that combats spiritual anorexia. It's called *The One Year Bible*. Kenneth Taylor, the translator of *The Living Bible*, has incorporated sections from the

Old and New Testaments, plus Psalms and Proverbs, into daily readings. By investing ten-to-fifteen minutes a day, you can read through the entire Bible in one year. And that will put any spiritual anorexic on the road to recovery.

As dangerous as spiritual anorexia is, there is another disorder that is even more dangerous. Bulimia is an eating disorder that is commonly known as the binge-and-purge syndrome. Usually, but not always, it is a young woman who will go on an eating binge and then attempt to get rid of the food either by vomiting or by the use of laxatives. Either way, the body is robbed of the nutrients that it so desperately needs.

Spiritual bulimia is knowing the Word of God without *doing* it. Or as James described, it is *hearing* the Word of God without doing it. Spiritual bulimia is characteristic of those who binge on truth: it can be through books, tapes, good Bible teaching, listening to a favorite communicator on the radio. That's why the spiritual bulimic appears to be so righteous. There's just one problem. The bulimic knows the truth but he doesn't apply it.

There is no man who consistently applies to his life all of the truth that he knows. Even as I write this I am thinking of situations where I have not put into practice what I know to be true. Perhaps your own inconsistencies are bothering you as well. If that is the case, then you are not bulimic. You are just human. The difference between the normal Christian man and the spiritual bulimic is that the bulimic is able to not apply the truth to his life and still feel at ease with himself. And that is the greatest disorder of all.

Physical Refueling

Bill Hybels

If your spiritual and emotional reserves are full and you still feel like hiding under your desk whenever you hear footsteps in the hall, you may need to check your physical fuel gauge.

One Wednesday night before Thanksgiving, I went to a rather lengthy meeting at church before driving with my family to Michigan. Although we did not get to bed there until five a.m., we had to get up early and start visiting with the relatives. I was in fine shape spiritually that Thanksgiving morning and in reasonable shape emotionally. But physically I was shot.

Every conversation was hard labor for me. Someone would tell a joke and I would think, "Don't be a jerk, Bill—laugh!" Relatives came to me, hoping for some input about a major decision they were making. But as I talked with them a little voice in my head was saying, "If you want an appointment, call my secretary. I'm sure there's an opening in June." I tried hard to hide how I really felt, but not until late Friday, after I had had time to recuperate physically, did I feel like myself again.

A lot of people these days are chronically run down physically. Most have no idea how much their physical condition undermines their attempts to love others. They fail to realize that it takes physical energy to listen, to serve, to confront, to rebuke. Not only are physically run-down people short on energy, but they tend to be easily irritated, critical, defensive, and negative. It is hard for them to love others, and it is equally hard for others to love them.

If you're spiritually and emotionally on track, but feel burned out, check your diet, your sleep, and your exercise. A few changes in your daily habits might be what you need to refuel your tank.

4

The Promises You Make to Your Wife

Gary Smalley and John Trent

Thereare two things on which wives depend in their husbands—two other marks of masculinity that are critical in
that basic building block of the family known as marriage:
independence and self-confidence.

INDEPENDENCE

There is a verse used in almost all wedding ceremonies that usually
gets as much attention as a distant relative standing in the reception
line. Yet within one sentence is a key to successful relationships
and a third mark of masculinity.

"For this reason a man shall 'leave' father and mother and
'cleave' to his wife."

The Scriptures note a stair-step progression between attraction
and intimacy. First comes "leaving," then "cleaving." First comes
independence, before there can be a healthy interdependence. Yet
many men who grow up in a feminized environment skip over
independence and opt for over-dependence. They settle for becoming "people-pleasers" rather than gaining a healthy sense of personal responsibility.

The popular word for "people-pleasers" today is the catch-word,
"co-dependent." Who are these people? They're the ones who,
when they're drowning, everybody else's life flashes in front of
their eyes!

Seriously, they're well-meaning people who push their nurturing skills far out of balance. So they become incredibly good at

anticipating and seeking to meet the needs of others, but they fail to come up with a direction or dream for themselves.

While this used to be a particularly feminine ailment, the ranks of co-dependent men are growing rapidly. And like their female counterparts, they become so unhealthily connected with others that they can't step beyond someone else's agenda to make up their own—or to say the simple word, "No."

Russ was a textbook example of this type of man. The youngest of three boys—the other two were deaf—he became the only connecting link between the mounting problems with the other children and a crumbling marriage.

Russ' father and mother wouldn't speak to each other directly. So for years they spoke through him. "Go tell your mother that I'm not going to be here tonight. . . ." "Oh, yea! Go back and tell your father that he's a *#+*##!!"

And as the only one in the family who could use sign language, he was also the interpreter for every conversation between his parents and two angry, rebellious brothers.

At seven and eight years of age, he was having to put out fistfights as well as verbal fires of scorn, hostility, and contempt that would have challenged an experienced clinical psychologist. And while he became an expert "people-pleaser" in trying to keep his family together, it came at a terrible price. He became so supersensitive to what it took to please everyone around him to avoid pain . . . it left no place for healthy personal growth. And it set him up for ulcers at work.

When Russ grew up and entered the work force, he was an exceptional employee. Just pile more and more on his desk and "good old Russ" would get it done (even if it meant coming in on most weekends). He made his boss look great, but he never once asked for or was given a significant raise or promotion.

And of course, his heightened sensitivity made him a real catch for his wife ("At last I've found a sensitive man!"). Only what she landed was a passive-aggressive man with a terrible problem—an inability to say no. Because Russ had grown up with almost no space between family members—if one person signaled a left turn, they all headed that direction. When you're a committed people-pleaser—afraid of losing relationships—the only direction you can turn is where everyone else wants to go. And soon this was true in his marriage as well.

If one night he really wanted spaghetti, they'd eat fish again if that's what she wanted. For almost a year he was convinced they needed a four-wheel drive. He bought all the auto magazines, even checked the paper each day for one they could get at a steal. But the weekend she said they had to get the new vehicle, he settled for the station-wagon she wanted—and another handful of Tums.

To say no to someone significant in his life was somehow unloving, unkind, unAmerican! But what it really was, was unhealthy. And the same thing is true in your life.

If you're up at all hours, accomplishing other people's projects because you can't say "no," then you're caught on the hook of "co-dependency." If you don't have the emotional breathing room to express your negative feelings directly to another person, then you've swallowed the line that "honesty is too fearful to handle." And if you don't get help in learning how to become more healthily independent, you'll end up with the sinker, and at the bottom in all your relationships.

Of course, as with assertiveness, independence lies on a continuum. There are also men who grow up with too much distance, and their exaggerated sense of personal space can ruin their relationships. But thankfully, in the middle of two extremes is the person of Christ who pictures the balance for us.

Jesus knew enough not to "entrust" Himself to the changing opinions of men who would crown Him one day and kill Him the next. He was closely bonded to His disciples, but He still remained "independent" enough to rebuke them for suggesting He forsake the cross. Even His daily dependence on the Father and the Holy Spirit wasn't an unhealthy "co-dependence" that blurred who He was, but a strengthening interdependence of the Three-in-One.

Can you make decisions without looking over your shoulder at Mom and Dad (not for counsel, but for permission)? Are you able to say, "I don't like that" to another person, without unreasonable fear that they'll say, "I don't like you"? And even if something you stand for isn't popular, do you have the inner strength to stand apart from the crowd and lean only on the rightness of your action?

If you seek to achieve that healthy independence, your wife will be able to know and respect the true you. She will see the real personality, the real decision-maker you can be. It will be the most important step you ever make toward a healthy interdependence with her. It will function best for both of you, though not by itself, but in combination with assertiveness, self-control, and another important attribute . . . self-confidence.

SELF-CONFIDENCE

We've now detailed three marks of masculinity: assertiveness, self-control, and independence. The next one is equally important as you look at keeping your promises to your wife.

Self-confidence is what everyone else in the locker room looks like they have before you hit the field for the big game, or get ready to hit your ball off the first tee. Actually, self-confidence is more than that look of determination, that purposeful step, the firmness in a handshake. It's that inner security of knowing who you are . . . and where you'll spend eternity.

Business books by the dozens confirm this necessary virtue in the work place. But a sense of confidence also needs to find a place in our personal lives.

What builds self-confidence? Primarily two things. And the foundation for both was laid long before we ever made it into the work force.

Standing Up to Cross-Examination
The first building block of self-confidence is something chiseled out of the word *credibility*. In court, a credible witness is one whose testimony can stand up to cross-examination. No inconsistencies or half-truths cut away at what is said from the stand.

In family life, a credible father is one whose walk matches his talk—who proves trustworthy time after time. This means that what you saw as a child can affect who you are today. So if credibility was missing from your background, it must become a priority if you're to take the highground of successful relationships.

But where do you begin to develop self-confidence? It begins with something that should be easy, but often becomes incredibly difficult for many to do—tell the truth.

Abraham Lincoln said, "I always tell the truth. . . . That way I only have to remember half as much."

Men who deal in secrets erode their self-confidence and often ruin their relationships as well. As long as we're hiding something, we're standing on thin ice. There's always the chance that some day, in some unexpected way, you'll pick up the phone and the secret will come out.

What happens to those who hide their secrets? In Proverbs 28:11, we read, "The wicked man flees though no one pursues, but the righteous are as bold as a lion."

Are you tired of feeling self-conscious? Worried for no apparent reason? Insecure? Fearful? Then take a hard look at your past. If there are secrets you're keeping, then expect to be chased down by negative emotions. But if it's confidence you desire, the very strength of a lion (and the Lion of Judah), then traffic in the truth at all times.

A Craftsman . . . Not a Workman

If the first building block of self-confidence is credibility, the second is just as important—credentials. Not necessarily the kind that put letters behind your name, but the kind that put a track record of excellence behind your efforts.

There is nothing that builds self-confidence quicker than excellence. Whether it's hitting the grade line right on the mark in your D-9 PushCat, getting a client's tax return to them early, or lining up seams on the wallpaper so they seem to disappear . . . excellence breeds confidence.

I (Gary) had the great opportunity to fly to Rumania several years ago with my oldest son, Greg. For several weeks, we had the privilege to minister to many in the underground church.

Today, people are worshipping out in the open there. But when General Ceausescu was in absolute power, we huddled in a different house church each night, with one person always near the door to listen for the footsteps of the secret police.

Coming from the United States, you noticed something about Rumania's repressive society right away. Namely, because there was no personal ownership of property, and no incentive for personal initiative, the standard of living and the state of the houses and cars was appalling.

In one house where we stayed, the electric wiring was exposed in several places, creating a dangerous situation for the young children who lived there. Three times they had different repairmen to come "fix" the problem, and each time the "solution" had worsened the problem.

At the end of that same trip, we crossed over the border into Germany. There, we stayed at the home of our group leader . . . a house that had been built by German workmen . . . or better, craftsmen.

The carved, oak front door looked like it could be a museum piece. The stained, spiral staircase was breathtaking. The perfectly lined baseboards looked like they had been laid out by computer, not by human hands. And the wooden cabinets fit together so perfectly that it looked like they were molded together.

The quality of craftsmanship gave the whole home a sense of stability and togetherness. And what excellence does for a home, it also builds into a life.

Some trades today still use the designation, "master" plumber or "master" electrician. When it comes to your job, could you put those credentials in front of your name? Better yet, if the work you do was laid out in the open for all to see . . . would it leave you as a "workman with nothing to be ashamed of"?

Recently, my wife and I (John) decided to defy the odds and jump into a full-scale renovation project. Now, we've done remodeling before. And frankly, we were looking forward to a major remodeling job like a good root canal. But what happened was an unbelievably pleasant surprise.

The general contractor we hired, a man named Brent Pemberton, is a craftsman in the best sense of the word. Detailed, patient, a great listener, and a positive example, he stresses excellence and cleanliness.

His exemplary attitude is illustrated well by what happened one late August day in the middle of the remodeling. He was in the process of knocking down our fireplace, block by mortared concrete block, to expand our small family room. It had to be

112 degrees in the shade when I pulled up in the driveway with a six-pack of diet sodas for him and his crew.

Brent was struggling with a wheelbarrow heaped full of heavy blocks on his way to the rented dumpster. With sweat dripping from his forehead, he gladly took one of the ice-cold pops I offered.

"I'm sorry you're having to battle the heat as well as that fireplace" I told him.

"Hey, don't worry John," he said. "This is great!"

"What's great?" I asked in disbelief.

"Are you kidding? Your fireplace is on the same side of the house as the dumpster. Usually I have to wheel this stuff around the whole house. Compared to that, this is great!"

And compared to anyone else we've ever seen, his work was great. On schedule, right on budget, and way over our highest expectations.

Perhaps Brent's commitment to excellence has something to do with why he is also in such high demand by the NBA! He has a small company on the side that builds the scorer's tables with the revolving ad boards that can be seen in the Boston Garden, the Chicago Bulls arena, and the new Phoenix Suns stadium, to name a few.

We were so spoiled when Brent finished his part of the job that we should have quit while we were ahead . . . and never hired the painters.

It's bad enough to paint wall-to-wall when you have two kids and a dog dodging the paint cans as they run through the house. But it's even worse when one group "finishes" and you have to hire another group to paint the whole inside all over again.

Yes, they were licensed, and bonded, and insured. But we found out that these things don't mean what they used to. After weeks of hassle, we finally gave up and paid again to have the job done right the second time around—this time by a craftsman.

When the dust settled, I had a talk with the first painting contractor. As a result of the fiasco at our house (and three other homeowners who strongly complained) he ended up firing three men on his crew who had been with him for a number of years. Why would he fire such loyal employees?

When he explained the seriousness of the complaints he'd

gotten about their work, they just said, "What's the problem? You got your money, didn't you?"

Many men are interested only in payday's golden egg. But they don't realize that if they've killed the goose during the week, there won't be any eggs for the weekend.

Self-confidence is built by credibility and credentials. It doesn't come by cutting corners on a job. It comes only to those who make a commitment to truthfulness and who have a passion for excellence, for a job well done.

If masculine independence lends the cornerstone of health to a marriage, then the steadiness of credibility and credentials—and the appropriate self-confidence that results, is the capstone. If healthy independence builds healthy interdependence, then a husband's self-confidence surely gives his wife a deeper sense of security. A healthy self-confidence will in turn transfer over to your wife and help her feel a similar self-confidence. In turn, it also gives her the security to allow her husband to lead the family. Needless to say, a healthy circle of emotional support between each of you will be a capstone on your marriage.

An independence leading to healthy interdependence, and self-confidence that leads to deep emotional support for and from your wife—these are important marks of masculinity.

Make a promise to your wife, and do yourself a favor at the same time. Be sensitive to your wife's need for a man who makes use of the positive effects of independence and self-confidence.

Learning to Live with Forgiveness

Ken Taylor

After six years of stove heat I spent a summer vacation digging out a crawl space beneath the house to install a Sears gas furnace that hung from the floor joists. As I dug, the children crawled away with buckets of dirt. The furnace had to go under the house because the only first floor closet already contained the water heater. It was a difficult summer because Margaret had no confidence in my ability to install the furnace properly and gave me no encouragement at all. The hardest part of the furnace job was trying to put the duct work into the crawl space where the floor joists were only about eighteen inches above the ground, a space filled with cobwebs, and in my overactive imagination, scorpions, tarantulas, and black widow spiders!

That gas furnace almost blew apart—or so it seemed to me—when I finally got it installed and tried to light it! The problem was that I misunderstood the instruction for lighting the pilot and the chamber was half-filled with gas when I lit a match. Fortunately neither the furnace nor I was hurt.

Margaret's unhappiness with me about installing the furnace was symptomatic of a growing tension between us. She was hurt by my indifference to our need for a larger house, and I felt her exasperation. But I always thought my ideas were better than hers, and she quietly resented this arrogance. There were no harsh words between us, but I became very defensive and was easily offended by any critical comment she made or even by ordinary remarks that I interpreted as criticism.

I find it painful now to look back and remember how I would

sulk in moody silence, sometimes for many hours. Margaret, unaware of having offended me, was perplexed. At times I would leave the house and walk for hours, seething, until my anger was spent. Perhaps even worse were mornings when I left for work without kissing her, saying only a stony goodbye as I left. Then I was in turmoil the rest of the day.

I knew I had no right to be resentful and angry, but I didn't know what to do. I knew the Scripture and deeply desired to obey it: "Husbands, love your wives, and be not bitter against them" (Colossians 3:19, KJV). And as one who believed in and practiced prayer, I was deeply branded by the apostle Peter's admonition to husbands to treat their wives properly, "that your prayers be not hindered" (1 Peter 3:7, KJV).

But what I wanted and longed for—steady peace and joy with my wife—seemed beyond my ability.

I remember taking a long walk the night I finally realized that this simply must not go on. There seemed to be two ways to respond to her criticism. One was to regard any criticism of me as a fault in her that I had to live with; it was unfortunate to have such a childish wife, but I would mentally pat her on the head and haughtily ignore this fault of hers. As soon as I said this to myself, however, I knew it was wrong and wouldn't work. That attitude would not expunge my bitterness. It would not qualify me as meeting the apostle Paul's criteria for godly living, and it would not qualify me for getting my prayers answered.

The other solution was one I could not bear. That was simply to forgive Margaret for criticizing me. But I rebelled against this. It was unfair. Why should I forgive her for hurting me—and sometimes I was deeply hurt? But I was absolutely serious with God on that long walk that night, and I was serious with Margaret, though she was not there. The situation must end, and since Margaret would not solve the problem by no longer criticizing me, I would have to take the lead by acknowledging her criticism as valid, then trying to learn from it, meanwhile forgiving her for hurting me.

As I came up the dark driveway to our home, I made my decision to acknowledge my fault; I rehearsed in my mind the remark she made two hours before, acknowledged that she was right, and forgave her for hurting me. I entered the house quietly, but no longer in silent anger, and spoke to Margaret as though nothing had happened. It was one of the hardest actions of my life—to allow myself to admit the fault she had alleged, and concurrently to say in my heart, "I forgive you," and mean it. But God helped me.

The next time a criticism came—a few days later, I suppose— I flared up internally as before but rushed out and prayed for help to accept and forgive, then I came back quieted a few minutes later. Not many days went by before I realized that the flareups took a shorter and shorter time to deal with, and they could finally be handled immediately. A few weeks later, Margaret remarked to me, "You are different from the way you were," and I knew the Lord's grace had prevailed, the spiritual battle of many years was ended, and Satan, who had conquered for so long, was himself conquered.

And when the turmoil ended, the grass could become fresh and green and flowers could grow and bloom—and they did.

The Promise to Pray with My Wife

John Yates

On an August day when I was half the age I am today, I made two promises that have changed my life more than I could ever have imagined. The one was to be a faithful, loving husband to the woman I married that day. The other was to have a talk with God, together as husband and wife, every night at bedtime. We had no idea how important the second promise would be in helping us to keep the first promise, as we prayed together for the first time as husband and wife in a romantic, honeymoon setting on the Florida coast.

Marriage is intended by God to be a partnership between three persons—husband, wife, and God. A brief daily meeting of the three, where sincere and honest communication takes place, goes a long way toward strengthening a successful, productive, and happy partnership for life.

My wife and I have since learned to pray together at any time, in any situation. But it was praying at bedtime that taught us how valuable prayer is to a marriage. Why?

1. We can't remain estranged from someone when we pray with them. We have to be reconciled to one another before we dare utter those words "Our Father" out loud together. Bedtime prayer together is a built-in safety valve that ensures we deal with any anger, friction, or hurt between ourselves and our mate. Before we speak to God together, we have to come together as one, at peace with one another. It requires at least some reconciliation if there has been estrangement.

2. Every time we pray together it adds one more layer of that divine, protective bonding material the Holy Spirit uses to strengthen the marriage and keep it secure. Like an additional coat of glue to bond two halves into one, sincere, honest, dependent prayer bonds us to God and to one another.

3. Prayer reminds us of what things are really most important to us at that moment. We can't pray well without thinking about what is most important in our minds *and* in her mind. It forces us to put ourselves in our mate's position, and think about how she is feeling, what she is most concerned about, what weighs on her. We do the same thing for ourselves before we pray. This helps us to know what is weighing heaviest on one another's hearts, what the other is most joyful or concerned about. Prayer builds communication.

4. Finally, praying with our wife humbles us, and reminds us of what and who is most important. It helps us keep perspective and comforts us when we are in need. It reminds us of our senior partner and His reassuring promise to care for us.

Your prayer together need not be long nor formal nor "religious." The two need not both pray aloud—just one is enough. All areas of need or concern needn't be covered. What matters most is that you as the husband see that the two of you take these few moments after your heads hit the pillow or on your knees at the bedside.

To be still before God.

To be reconciled if anything has come between you.

To bring to God, simply but genuinely, the things you know you need Him to help you handle, to thank Him, and to recommit yourselves to His care and to His way.

Many nights I have been severely tempted to turn away from my wife into my own selfishness or anger, but the promise to God to pray every night has forced me to come back to her and to God. This is a promise well worth keeping.

What Can You Own?

Donald R. Harvey

As a marriage counselor, most of my professional time is spent working with couples in conflict. As you can guess, I've heard about everything imaginable. Though the actual stories and events presented by couples have varied, there are some predictable characteristics which seem to accompany the early sessions. One theme is the tendency to justify or excuse any personal wrongdoings.

Sometimes this justification takes the form of blaming a mate. For example, in the case of an affair: "If you'd been a better spouse, I wouldn't have looked elsewhere." When there has been physical abuse: "I wouldn't have hit you if you hadn't driven me to it." At other times, other avenues of justification are selected. For example, "That's the way I was raised," or "That's just the way I am."

Though natural and predictable, this tendency toward justification (somehow justifying wrong behavior) is not helpful. Therefore, I immediately begin challenging these positions by asking questions: "What can you own?" and "What has been your contribution to this deteriorating marriage?" I find that mates generally do not like this line of questioning. That's not why they're in my office. They would rather talk about the other's faults and limitations than their own. But reconciliation will not begin until each one is willing to stop blaming the other and start the accepting. There has to be an ownership of personal wrongdoing.

We have this natural tendency to dodge any personal responsibility for wrongdoing. Biblical examples go as far back as the Garden of Eden. Genesis 3 records the conversation between God and the first family. When God asked Adam why he had disobeyed Him, he said it was because of "the woman" (verse 12). And when He asked Eve the same question, she said it was because of "the serpent" (verse 13). It is so easy for our misbehavior to be someone or something else's fault.

Real men accept responsibility for their behavior. They own what is rightfully theirs to own. Granted, there may be some legitimacy to their complaints. Like a poster in a colleague's office noted, "Just because you're paranoid doesn't mean people aren't out to get you." There may be truth to your accusations. But as I frequently remind my adolescent son, "There's no right reason for doing the wrong thing."

Reconciliation begins with, "I'm wrong." It is then followed by several other essential elements (remorse, changed behavior, forgiveness, etc.). But reconciliation always begins with ownership. What part of the failure can you own? It is with a willingness to accept responsibility for your behavior that true masculinity is displayed in a marriage.

The Image of Christ

Ken Brown

M any years ago a pastor friend and I were discussing women, and I said I believed that all women were looking for the same things in a man. Since my friend seemed to have some reservations concerning this idea, we decided to see what we could find out about it.

Our first project was to interview two women. We decided that we wanted these women to be different in as many ways as we could possibly find. The first was a Christian, twenty-two years old, single, raised in what we considered an excellent home. The second did not profess to be a Christian, was thirty-seven years old, divorced twice, the product of a broken home, and raised by an abusive stepfather. In separate interviews we asked both women what kind of man they wanted for a husband. Trying not to lead them to any conclusions, we asked them to answer our questions as honestly as they could, and found only slight differences between what both women desired! Both women wanted:

•A man who was honest and could earn their confidence and trust.
•A man who was sensitive and caring, truly interested in their needs.
•A man who was loyal, always willing to protect them from those who didn't have their best interest at heart.
•A man who was faithful, never betraying the bond between them.
•A man whose love was freely given and unconditional,

letting the woman enjoy acceptance.
• A man who cherished the woman, acknowledging her value and importance to him.

Even though the course of their lives had been quite opposite and the differences between the two women were obvious, the desire and cry of their hearts were very much the same. They longed to experience the image of Christ in a relationship with a man.

Since that time, I've talked to hundreds of women, and I've seen the same desire I saw years ago in the first two. Men, you need to understand that it doesn't matter what you now think about your wife. You may think she's hateful, angry, critical, or just plain hard to please. But let me suggest this for your honest consideration: maybe she's frustrated because she has yet to experience an intimate relationship with a man who is honestly striving to be the image of Christ. Maybe she's more than just a little disappointed because you've given her reason to doubt your commitment, or you've been insensitive, disloyal, unfaithful, lacking in self-control, demanding, or unappreciative.

Remember, no woman has ever gone into a marriage looking forward to a relationship with a man who is going to frustrate and disappoint her. What she's looking for is the image of Christ.

Every man who contemplates marriage needs to realize that making a commitment to a woman must include making a commitment to God to conform to the image of Christ. The image of Christ is the standard God imprints on the soul of every woman. She may consciously decide to lower this standard and accept less, but it will not be what she wants. Less than the standard will not make her happy. Less than the standard will not fulfill her.

Men, don't try to establish your own standards, it won't work: Nothing other than God's standard will do.

Putting Aside Your Pride

Dennis Rainey

It can be pretty difficult for a man to resolve a conflict with his wife. To do so requires humility, the willingness to take the initiative, and the ability to both ask for and grant forgiveness. It also requires the ability to set aside your own "rights."

This lesson hit home for me one day when I was preparing to leave town and speak at a conference. I came home to a wife who had spent a hard day with the kids—a very hard day. But while I wanted to reach out and help Barbara, I was just too busy preparing to leave.

Just as I picked up the phone to make one last important call, she said, "Please don't get on the phone right now. I really want to talk to you; and if you get on that phone, I'm going upstairs."

I could tell she was hurting and needed to talk to me, but I had to make that call. So I hastily dialed the number. With disappointment on her face, Barbara disappeared upstairs. More than a few minutes went by before the phone conversation ended. Then my mother called and we talked another twenty minutes.

My mother and I finally hung up, and I stayed a few more minutes, cleaning up the kitchen and watching a small TV set we have on the counter. The show was so interesting I sat for a moment to see how it would end.

So there I was, watching television, when Barbara walked in. Obviously, my stock didn't go to blue chip status at that moment. She didn't notice her kitchen was clean. All she saw was her husband glued to the TV set when he knew she had been waiting to talk to him.

By the time we got to our bedroom, the temperature seemed to be about forty degrees below zero. Our conversation opened on a note especially familiar to many couples. With keen male insight, I said, "What's wrong?"

"Nothing!"

"Sweetheart," I said, "you knew I was trying to get up here."

Barbara brushed that comment angrily away and said, "And you knew I wanted to talk because it has been a hard day."

"Well, do you want to talk or not?" I asked, showing that I was getting a little perturbed.

No answer. By now my eyelids were getting heavy and I was doing my best to hold them open as she nursed our newborn baby, Laura. Then, when she finished feeding the baby, she put her in her crib, took a pillow, and hit me on top of the head!

It wasn't a very playful whack, and I got the message loud and clear. Smarting with anger, I took the pillow, propped it under my head, and rolled over to stare at the wall.

Then Barbara said, "Don't you want to talk?"

"I tried to a while ago."

There was a long silence. Finally, I gathered enough presence of mind to say, "You know, sweetheart, neither one of us is doing real well in this relationship at the moment, and we should reschedule this conflict for tomorrow because we are not getting anywhere. Why don't we just go to sleep?"

"Okay."

The next morning things were still a little tense when we sat down to talk, but before I left for the conference I admitted to Barbara that I had been insensitive by not coming upstairs when she had given me her first distress signal. "I should have seen you really meant it. I blew it, and I'm sorry."

"Well, I'm sorry, too. It was pretty childish to whack you with a pillow, but I was hurt—and finding you watching TV was the last straw."

We talked a while longer, and then I had to leave to catch my plane. But by the time I left, we were both feeling a lot better because we had used a key principle of resolving conflict: Even though we didn't feel like it, we were willing to put aside our pride and forgive each other as an act of the will.

Real Men Don't

Steve Farrar

D o you remember the book *Real Men Don't Eat Quiche*? It had some humorous one-liners on the definitive charac-teristics of a real man. I also have a one line, but it's not meant to be funny. Real men don't commit adultery.

Adultery in America is an epidemic of staggering proportions. It's an epidemic that for the most part used to afflict only those outside the body of Christ. No longer. This epidemic has not only found its way inside the church, but has wormed its way up to the highest echelons of church leadership.

There's something strange about this epidemic other than its rolling virtually unchecked through the Body of Christ. What is strange is that we don't call it "adultery."

Let's cut the doubletalk. Let's put the cards on the table. Let's call adultery what it is. In the way of the family, adultery is treason. But we don't call it treason. We have developed a more refined and sophisticated term. Adultery has become an "affair."

When a man leaves his wife and children for another woman and acts as impulsively as an aroused junior high kid on his first date, it's not an "affair." It's adultery.

Real men don't have affairs because real men are responsible. Real men keep their commitments: even when their personal needs are not being met the way they would hope; even when they are disappointed in their wives for some reason.

I remember a number of years ago watching Phyllis George interview Dallas Cowboy superstar Roger Staubach. It was a typi-cal, dull sort of interview until Phyllis blindsided the quarterback with this question: "Roger, how do you feel when you compare yourself with Joe Namath, who is so sexually active and has a different woman on his arm every time we see him?"

We've all seen Staubach keep his cool in pressure game situations, and the tension in the air this time was just as great. But once again, Staubach kept his cool.

"Phyllis," he said calmly, "I'm sure I'm just as sexually active as Joe. The difference is that all of mine is with one woman."

Touchdown! Roger hit the end zone with that comeback. Real men don't commit adultery. A real man sticks with one woman. Period.

The Sensitive Man and Romance

Charles Stanley

The sensitive man knows there is a distinct difference between sex and love. Sex should include love, but often it does not. Many popular songs portray love as being little more than a kind of animal lust, beneath the dignity of personalities made in the image of God. Far from being love, illicit sex is a sin by which a man "destroyeth his own soul" (Proverbs 6:32, KJV).

Not only single people are ignorant of true love. Married couples can express hostility or contempt in the sex act. Sex is the expression of many things—but not according to God's plan. As it is the deepest intimacy between committed husband and wife, its perversion becomes the highest travesty against love.

A woman would like to live her whole life experiencing romantic love because God made women to be loved. If you have lost all traces of your romantic days of courtship, you are a big loser. Sex, love, and romance are not always synonymous but they can be, and they are for the complete man.

Romantic loves reaches out in little ways, showing attention and admiration. Romantic love remembers what pleases a woman, what excites her and what surprises her. Its action whispers: You are the most special person in my life.

Someone said in infancy a woman needs love and care, in childhood she needs fun, in her twenties she needs romance, in her thirties she needs admiration, in her forties she needs sympathy, and in her fifties she needs cash! The needs of a whole woman would more likely be the same in her fifties as in her infancy: love and care. This never changes.

5

The Promises You Make to Your Family

Gary Smalley and John Trent

W e've now looked at four marks of masculinity. The combination of these four traits nailed together can give us the strength we need to live out a fifth trait, no matter what the cost.

The most important promise every family needs from its primary leader—Dad—also happens to be the final mark of masculinity. We've looked at four of these most important masculine character traits already: assertiveness, self-confidence, independence, and self-control. All of these must work together for a man to become a Christlike picture of masculinity.

In the "Promises You Make to Yourself" chapter of this book, theologian and counselor Larry Crabb gave us a challenge to become radically "other-centered" in all of our relationships, especially with our wives. This focus on *others first* is a critical part of family life as well. And it will lead you toward that fifth mark of a Christlike man—stability.

STABILITY

Stability, it turns out, is perhaps the number-one hope of a wife for her family life. Unfortunately, too often we men fail to recognize the critical need for stability in our own lives, and the consequential benefits it brings to our families. It gives our wives security; it lends our children a safe haven from harm's way. For the alternative to stability, to being a man who can "stay put," is a miserable existence.

Second Lt. Bobo was already over the halfway point of going home after ten months of combat duty in Vietnam. He was a platoon leader in I Company, 3rd Battalion, 9th Marines. Often leading missions in the "bush," and frequently in the midst of a firefight, he had earned his men's respect. But on March 30, 1967, he would earn a nation's highest honor.

Just barely twenty-four, Bobo ducked his head and jumped out of his helicopter when it touched the ground. His objective was Hill 70, in Quang Tri Province, from which his platoon was to set up an ambush site.

For a short time, they struggled through the elephant grass toward their position without incident. But what they were experiencing was the calm before a deadly storm. A large force of front line NVA regulars had massed to pull off their own ambush. Lt. Bobo's men were about to walk right into it.

Their lead elements saw several NVA soldiers and opened fire. But all that accomplished was to pinpoint their own position and signal the enemy to open fire.

In presighted killing zones, the hidden NVA poured machine gun and mortar fire onto the men on Hill 70. Many of them died before ever firing a return shot in that first firestorm of bullets.

Lt. Bobo shouted orders above the din of battle, positioning his troops to return fire and calling in air support. Murderous fire was coming from several machine gun emplacements that were ripping his men to pieces. When a mortar round knocked out a Marine rocket team, Lt. Bobo ran forward and took over their position. He directed the firing of round after round at the enemy strongpoints, with bullets shredding the ground around him.

He was still firing when a mortar shell landed nearby, showering him with shrapnel and blowing off the lower part of his right leg. First Stg. Raymond Rogers crawled up to his commander, telling him, "You've got to go to the rear, Lieutenant. You've got to stop that bleeding. I'll cover you.

"Crawl back, Lieutenant. Please!"

But Lt. Bobo refused. "Just tie my leg off. Now! And give me all the shotgun ammo you've got. Then help me to the ridge." The sergeant did what he was commanded and pulled a web belt tightly around his commanding officer's leg as a tourniquet.

Bobo had judged correctly what was to happen next. After the first devastating machine gun and mortar attack, the enemy was preparing for a mass ground assault to overrun Bobo's position and massacre his remaining troops. From where they were, they couldn't form an effective enough defensive perimeter.

"Pull back," Bobo shouted. "Everybody back," he ordered his men—all of them— back down the hill. As Sgt. Rogers helped gather the men, a machine-gun toting NVA soldier suddenly stood over him, wounding Rogers and several others.

"Boom!" blasted Bobo's shotgun, spinning the enemy soldier around and knocking him to the ground.

"Get back," he yelled. "Get back."

But Bobo stayed put.

Those were the last orders Bobo would give his men. Dragging their wounded to safety, the remaining members of his platoon repositioned themselves farther down the hill.

Bobo raised to a half-sitting position, jamming his wounded leg into the ground to try to stop the flow of blood. As the NVA charged down the hill, Bobo met the brunt of the attack. His men heard the boom, boom, boom of his shotgun as the enemy swarmed over the hill until finally his gun fell silent.

Lt. Bobo had faced the brunt of their charge and bought the rest of his men the needed time to pull back to a more defensible position, but at the cost of his own life.

When reinforcements arrived, the Marines fought their way back up the hill. There they found their commander. Fallen . . . but not to be forgotten.

For his sacrificial courage and extreme heroism, his family received our nation's highest honor—the Congressional Medal of Honor. Lt. Bobo was a man who was willing to "stay put," no matter what the cost.

We share this story because we need more men like Lt. Bobo, particularly today, when there is such a battle raging over the lives and hearts of many families.

The ultimate mark of a man is that he is willing to "stay put" when the odds aren't good, rather than turning and running from his wife and children when the times get tough, and the cost is high.

We are absolutely sick of talking of men who have "lost their feelings" for their spouse and decided it's simply easier to get a new one. Of course it is! At least in the short run. But soon that newfound person who is so "easy" to love will pile on just as many demands . . . until it's time for family number three . . . or four.

If we are truly men, then we'll dig in when the times get tough. We'll stay with the pain and be "trained" by it, rather than relying on our "feelings" and breaking our promises—at least if we're serious about being like Christ.

Jesus could have cut and run at the garden. Between the temple walls, where the palace guards came from, and the hilltop of Gethsemane was a large gully called the Kidron Valley. It gave Jesus a perfect hilltop view of the temple wall . . . and the gate the soldiers coming for Him would be coming from. Watching the troops move down the slope and up toward the garden, there was plenty of time to flee. Yet Jesus "endured the cross, suffering the shame," that we might be won back to Him.

If the analogy seems a bit strained, remember the words of Ephesians 5:25: "Husbands, love your wives just as Christ loved the church and gave himself up for her."

We may not want to go into counseling again to seek solutions to our problems. We may have found someone at work who didn't come from such a "dysfunctional" background as our wife. But we will not find true masculinity if we don't hold our ground and fight for what is right.

Do you change jobs nearly as often as you change your socks? Have you moved your family five times in the last six years? Are you feeling those same hopeless feelings with your second marriage that ended the first?

It's not popular to stay put anymore, but then it's never easy to be courageous. Your wife needs you to stay. Your children will be damaged if you don't. But *you* need to stay most of all, to keep from adding an even larger hole to your own heart.

Promise your family a stable home; you can start by giving them a stable Dad.

Fathers and Daughters

John E. Brown III

Then our sons in their youth will be like well-nurtured plants,
and our daughters will be like pillars carved to adorn a palace.
(Psalm 144:12)

I have yet to reconcile myself to the diminishing role of parents in the lives of their children. One author equates our responsibility to that of a kite flyer who slowly lets the string out as the kite flies higher and higher, eventually setting it free to sail into the upper atmosphere.

Such grace and granted freedom are particularly hard between fathers and daughters, I think.

The oldest of my four female progeny is now twelve, and very much the young lady. Our youngest daughter just turned three. That means she now knows bathroom etiquette—a length in the kite string I found *very* easy to let out.

On the other hand, it seems unjust in the extreme that a father and mother should spend the best twenty years of their lives (not to mention a small fortune in clothes and manicures) cultivating these little flowers only to see them carried away by marriage, a career, or both.

I guess that I will be one of those brusque and stern fathers who greets young gentlemen callers at the door with an icy glare. My sentiments at their probable point of matrimony will be like those of my fellow college president and the former head of Youth for Christ, USA, Jay Kesler, who said, "Giving a daughter away in marriage is like handing a beautiful, expensive, Stradivarius violin over to a gorilla."

If my father-in-law had similar thoughts twenty years ago, he hid them well. To his credit, he never once gave me the "hairy ape" treatment as I crouched on the porch swing with his fair-haired second daughter.

The father-daughter relationship is especially important to the psychology of child development and adult maturity. Dr. Paul Faulkner, a well-known marriage and family counselor and professor from Abilene Christian University in Texas, made special note of this fact during a recent address to a group of Wal-Mart associates in Ft. Smith, Arkansas. In addition to his emphasis on interpersonal skills and motivators to human performance, Dr. Faulkner counseled the 200-plus employees and spouses on the importance of healthy family relationships.

"Fathers, hug your daughters," advised Dr. Faulkner. Daughters need this affirmation and affection from a father, or grandfather for that matter. Dr. Faulkner noted that fathers sometimes begin to hold back physical expressions of their love because of mixed emotions as they view their teenage daughter's budding womanhood.

"This is perfectly natural," counseled Dr. Faulkner. A proper understanding by the father of these emotions will allow an appropriately affectionate relationship with his daughter.

Fathers who cannot deal with these emotions ought to seek counseling. The delicate nature of the growing young woman can be irreparably altered by either an abusive relationship with the father or the unnatural absence of the father's demonstrations of caring for her.

"Studies show that girls who have a lot of appropriate, affectionate touching from their parents, and especially from their fathers, do not usually get married as young as those whose fathers ignore them," echoes Jim Conway of Talbot Theological Seminary. "Appropriate affection meets their need for physical closeness and causes them to take time to make a serious marriage choice."

In other words, if you do not want your daughter to run off with a gorilla, Dad, express your love often and include a hug now and then.

If this technique is not applied, then Kesler, Faulkner, and Conway would suggest that you plan on supplying large quantities of bananas at the wedding reception.

Fathers and Daughters

Steve Brown

B oth of our daughters are now married. Their new husbands are fine young men who love Christ and love them. We prayed for these young men before our daughters were born, and we are thankful to the Lord for the wonderful gifts they are to our daughters and to our family.

But two weddings in a little over three months? That is almost more than a father of daughters can bear. People ask me if I have seen the movie *Father of the Bride*. Of course not! That would be like watching a video of hell before you went there.

To be perfectly honest with you, I would have been far more sympathetic to fathers (and mothers) of brides over the twenty-eight years I was a pastor if I had only known what they were going through. They always seemed to be so happy and together. Now, having gone through it myself, I know they were happy, but it was a bittersweet sort of happiness. And anybody who looks together during the wedding of their son or daughter deserves an Academy Award.

I wake up each morning and thank the Lord that I don't have three daughters.

Did I cry? Are you crazy? Of course I cried. I didn't "blubber," but this crusty, old preacher did cry. I cried because of the memories. I cried because the ceremonies were so filled with meaning. I cried because God had been so faithful. I cried because I knew that, after this day, nothing would ever be the same.

Now it's over. All the preparations, all the time, all the plans, all the cooking (Anna prepared for both receptions by cooking months in advance), all the emotional drain, all the excitement and joy of two marriages are behind us. God has made our two daughters one with two young men He picked out especially for them. And now it's all behind us.

And for the first time in a long while, I have some time to stop for a few moments and reflect on what happened. For the first time in a long time I can stop for a moment and ask why I was so emotionally involved—why I felt so filled with joy and, at the same time, sort of sad. It's all settled down now, and I have some time to pray and think. I thought I would share with you some things I've been thinking.

First, I've thought of God's faithfulness. The psalmist wrote, "Thy faithfulness endures to all generations" (Psalm 119:90). It really does, you know?

That, of course, doesn't mean that God's faithfulness always includes happiness, or success, or even *our* faithfulness. But, as I look back over the years, I see God's hand in every circumstance, in every choice, and in every change. He has always been there—loving, caring, forgiving, and sometimes, admonishing and chastening. There hasn't been one circumstance that He hasn't ordained and controlled. There hasn't been one time in my life that He didn't share. The weddings of our daughters were not the exceptions.

It started long before our children were born—long before the world was made. God decided to have a people called after His name. He created all that is and brought forth His family—the people of God. He made a covenant with His people and promised to hold them and to love them throughout eternity. And He promised to get them home.

Paul likened marriage to the marriage of Christ to His people. Paul writes, "Husbands, love your wives, just as Christ also loved the church and gave himself up for her, that he might sanctify and cleanse her with the washing of water by the word, that he might present her to himself a glorious church, not having spot or wrinkle or any such thing, but that she should be holy and without blemish" (Ephesians 5:25-27).

As I watched our two daughters standing to make their vows before God and His people, I thought of them . . . but I also thought of Him. I thought of His promises and His love. I thought of His goodness. I was thankful.

Secondly, I've thought about the uncertainty of the future. The preacher wrote, "The race is not to the swift, nor the battle to the strong, nor bread to the wise, nor riches to men of understanding, nor favor to men of skill; but time and chance happen to them all" (Ecclesiastes 9:11).

There really aren't any sure things in the world. Jennifer and Jimmy, Robin and Mike are all young. There are stars in their eyes and dreams in their hearts. They have plans . . . big plans for the future. They haven't faced all that life can do to extinguish the stars and stifle the dreams. They don't know about the tears yet. They don't know the circuitous ways their lives will take.

But they don't know about the new dreams, either. They have not experienced the way God fulfills His will in the commitments they have made. They don't know about the unexpected successes, the surprising gifts the Father gives, or about the laughter and the joy that He will give them in the years He has ordained for their marriage.

Watching these young people begin a whole new life together, I was moved deeply as I thought about the road they would walk. There was not only a feeling of giving daughters away, but also the sense of giving all four of these young people I love into the hands of another loving Father who would walk them through the multitude of changes—some good and some bad, some painful and some joyful—that the future will hold. I felt a sense of relief as I realized that I could trust them to another Father who will watch over them long after Anna and I have gone home. He loves them more than Anna and I love them—and we love them a lot.

Thirdly, I've thought about commitment and love. Paul wrote the Philippians that they should be the "children of God without fault in the midst of a crooked and perverse generation, among whom you shine as lights in the world" (Philippians 2:14).

We live in a frightening time. There is a sense in which it will be harder for our daughters and their husbands than it was for Anna and me. This will be a difficult time to start a family, to remain faithful to Christ, and to make a witness for Him in a fallen world. A lot of the advantages we had with them (a culture largely favorable to our values, strong affirmation in the media to the verities of the Christian faith, and a cultural base that affirms rather than destroys) are disappearing today.

A missionary home on furlough told me about the difficulties she had faced in her call to the destructive and harsh culture where she was serving. I asked her what she was going to do when she returned. She smiled and said, "I'm going back to plant flowers in hell."

That's what these young people are doing. In the midst of a time of shattered hopes and harsh realities, they are making a statement of faith and hope. Lewis Carroll in *Alice in Wonderland* has Alice saying, "Cheshire-Puss, would you tell me, please, which way I ought to go from here?" The cat replies, "That depends a good deal on where you want to get to." These young people are heading to the future of hope—planting flowers, if you will, in a bad place—and they have made a good statement about God and the future.

Fourthly, I've thought about the changes. The psalmist prayed, "Indeed, You have made my days as handbreadths, and my age is nothing before You; Certainly every man at his best state is but vapor. Surely every man walks about like a shadow; surely they busy themselves in vain; he heaps up riches, and does not know who will gather them." Then the psalmist adds, "And now, Lord, what do I wait for? My hope is in you" (Psalm 39:5-7, NKJV).

How fast time flies!

It seems like only yesterday when Anna and I stood before a pastor and made our vows. It was only a blink ago that our daughters were born. Then I turned around and found the time was gone, the little girls with the frilly dresses, giggles, and childlike questions were grown up and beginning families of their own. I don't know where the time went . . . and there is some sadness in that. It is the sadness of knowing that memories are just that—past memories to which one can't return.

And Anna and I are starting a new life too. We are establishing new memories and new ways of doing things. We have made plans and are looking forward to what God has planned for the future. We are getting reacquainted again, traveling together and feeling free of the constant responsibility that parents feel for their children. Things are a whole lot quieter now, and our lives are less rushed than they were. The house seems bigger than it did, and it is a lot quieter. There are empty places that were filled with the laughter of our daughters. Sometimes there is loneliness. The empty nest and vacant bedrooms are filled with memories.

Isn't that bad? No, that's good.

How do we like it? I'm glad you asked. We like it a whole lot!

Family Finances

Don Osgood

D r. Louis Kopolow, staff psychiatrist with the National Institute of Mental Health, discussed the emotional cost of inflation and recession in a government document. "With the coming of rampant inflation, tight money, oil shortages, and unemployment, the mood of the country changed drastically. Gone were the optimism and the confidence that money would always be available for bigger and better plans.

"For the individual citizens," he continued, "the change in the economy has created a feeling of insecurity, financial strain, and fear of the future." Dr. Kopolow then summarized what many Americans have come to realize. "For the first time in their lives, millions of Americans are losing confidence in their ability to achieve a more prosperous future or even to maintain their present economic condition."

Harvey Brenner of Johns Hopkins University completed a study of psychiatric admissions in New York State over the past 127 years and found that admissions to psychiatric hospitals increased whenever economic conditions turned downward. He found that economic stress causes a rise in alcoholism among working-class families and a rise in suicide among families in higher economic levels. He also found that males ages forty-five to sixty are admitted to hospitals for emergency treatment of emotional distress in significantly higher numbers during economic downturns.

Unemployment takes its toll, not only because people need money, but also because people lose their social place in the community, their sense of security, and the prestige they have learned to expect. "In the long-term phase," according to Dr. Kopolow, "substantial unemployment or belt tightening can produce strained family relationships."

What can a family do when economic stress becomes a reality? Our changing economy has become such a difficult thing to foretell that the fear of the future which Dr. Kopolow mentions is a recurring thing. It seems that every few weeks there is a new report about a hoped-for rise in the economy, followed by a prediction of a downturn. One person put the stressful feeling that results from such uncertainty this way: "These days when you see the light at the end of the tunnel, you have to be careful. It might be a freight train."

Where most of us are concerned, economic stress boils down to family finances. The problem is that we let our family finances get out of hand. First thing we know we're on a treadmill. It's no longer a case of joy from beating the system. The system has the upper hand. The little snowball at the top of the hill has become a smothering giant as it rolls down the hill toward us. That's the stressful predicament we get into with family finances. But there is a way out.

Actually, there are two ways out, and both of them should be used at the same time. One is to do all the simple but helpful things that will immediately change the family expense habits. Stop the flow of money or "profits" out the back door. The other is to look for the spiritual cause and set it straight. As farfetched as that may seem, there is often a spiritual problem at the bottom of the mounting pile of unpaid family bills.

The stress that comes from financial trouble can have a spiritual root, or a lack of it. Here are some of the underlying roots of financial distress:

Greed

Pretty tough label, isn't it? But we might as well call them as we see them. Acquiring more and more for ourselves—whether it is money or possessions—adds up to the same thing. Sometimes greed starts out with measuring the quality of life by the possessions we have. Two cars, a boat, a summer cottage, or a travel trailer are neither good nor bad. It's when we "need" them and can't afford them but get them anyway that gets us in the end. Measurement of life by our possessions or things is a root of distress.

Self-Love
The reason love of possessions is wrong is that it is the way we get trapped into preoccupation with ourselves. Real love looks out for someone, wishes good for someone, gives to someone. But love of possessions is loving ourselves, taking care of us, wishing good for us, giving to us. A family where each one is acquiring something just for self is a bankrupt family, whether or not the money has run out. And it usually won't be long before the money runs out. If we truly love someone, we are willing to deny ourselves.

Lack of Priorities
Sometimes financial difficulties come from lack of interest in the future. The old saying, "If you don't know where you're going, any road will get you there," has some truth in it. Up to a point. But most of us do care, when we stop to think about it. Some advance planning is necessary if we are to reduce financial stress in the family, including financial stress that comes when the person who is responsible for handling financial and business details dies. The most difficult day in family life is when death occurs, and that is complicated when nothing is in order.

The message of Jesus to those who are caught in the grip of financial worry is a simple one: "Do not be worried," He said. Then He asked one of the more profound questions in life: "Which one of you can live a few more years by worrying about it?" (Luke 12:25, TEV). What Jesus implied was that we can actually increase our financial and physical health at the same time.

The Only Truly Consistent Father

Ken R. Canfield

I f you are looking for an immovable standard by which to order your life, what better choice for a reference point than the "Father of the heavenly lights, who does not change like shifting shadows" (James 1:17)?

In fact, it is even a sign of an effective father when he leads his child to a point where he can say: "My son, I've done my best to lead a consistent life before you, to be a reliable reference whereby you can find your place in the world. But, as you know, there are things I don't know and mistakes that I make. I do my best, but if you choose me as the center of your universe, you will eventually find yourself lost. Let me fulfill my most important duty as a reference point by introducing you to a more stable, more reliable reference. I have been your earthly father, but now I want you to accept a heavenly Father and map out your life according to Him."

It's like our earthly fathers are a point on the coastline. If they are consistent, we have good reference points which guide us as we travel into the heart of the continent. Once inland, we discover the Capital City, and suddenly we know we've truly found it. All roads lead here. Everything is governed and defined by this point on the map. Now the entire continent makes sense. In the Middle Ages, men thought that the earth was the center of the universe and that all heavenly spheres revolved around it. This knowledge was sufficient to explain the moon's revolutions, and it also interested men in the study of the sun, which warms and feeds the earth. But then a scientist named Galileo studied the sun enough to conclude that it was actually the center of the solar system and that all planets, including the earth, made their revolutions around it. Some redrawing of the mental maps had to take place, but then it all made sense. The universe became a much more vast and awesome place, and our maps were more useful. For instance, we could finally map time and produce accurate calendars.

If you are a victim of inconsistency, God wants to become the new reference point in your life. He is offering Himself as your heavenly Father.

The Love of a Father

Jay Carty

I'm from Missouri. And I'm as stubborn as a Missouri mule. You thought as much and you were correct. We have some traditional Missouri Ozarks sayings in our household. They come from my dad. "Blinking like a toad in a hailstorm" is one. "Screaming like a smashed cat" is another. Or how about, "Nervous as a long-tailed cat in a room full of rockers"?

Missouri is the "show me" state. "The proof is in the puddin" is a saying that must have originated there. In Missouri the bottom line is the bottom line. Talk's cheap. Missourians reserve their judgment until they see action.

God must be from Missouri. He said that faith without works is dead (James 2:20). In other words, if you're a Christian, it ought to show.

One of the greatest days of my life came as a junior-higher when I came home from school depressed again. The kids had been talking about what their dads did for a living. My dad was a "bookmaker," and made his living bookin' horses and running a poker parlor.

When my father asked me what was wrong, I told him of my embarrassment regarding what he did. It was a Friday.

My dad was an honest gambler. So honest, in fact, his poker chips were legal tender at most of the markets and restaurants in our little town. He would make the rounds every Wednesday to redeem his chips.

But on that Friday he gave his notice. On Monday he collected all his chips, settled up, and began a legitimate business from which he would retire ten years later.

I never had to ask if my dad loved me or not. He gave up thousands of dollars a week, back when a thousand dollars was a lot of money. And he did it for the respect of his son and out of his love for him. He didn't just tell me he loved me, he showed it. The proof of his love was in what he did.

How much do dads who never show their sons or daughters how much they love them, really love them? Nobody knows—neither the dad nor the child. Only God. Lip service is not proof. Actions speak louder than words. The proof is in the puddin'.

Stop on a Dime

Jerry B. Jenkins

I sat near a mother and her preschool daughter in the Allentown, Pennsylvania, airport, eager to get home to my own family. Standing near us in the busy gate area was a middle-aged couple in animated conversation. As they chatted, the man pulled his hands from his pockets to gesture and a dime slipped out and bounced on the floor, rolling near his feet.

Neither the man nor his wife noticed, but the little girl and her mother did. The girl made a move for the dime, but the mother grabbed her arm. "I want that dime, Mommy," the girl whispered.

What an opportunity to teach this child ethics, fairness, and courtesy!

"I know," her mother said, giggling. "Wait till they walk away."

"He doesn't see it!" the girl said, fighting against her mother's grip.

"Just wait, honey," she said. "As soon as he leaves, you can have it."

When the older couple began to move away, I picked up the dime. "Excuse me, sir. You dropped this."

The man looked incredulous. "Hey, thanks a lot!"

I wasn't trying to be self-righteous or smug. A dime might seem insignificant, but I grieved for that child and the values she was learning. I could only hope her saucer-eyed look indicated she wished *she* had given the dime back to the man.

There was no question about the young mother's tight-lipped scowl. She wished I'd minded my own business. I wished her daughter *was* my business. I'm still kicking myself for not saying,

"Great job of parenting. I hope your daughter doesn't grow up to be an accountant. Or a civic leader. Or a mother like you."

Mercy—it's better I kept my mouth shut.

Who's Teaching Our Children?

Fran Sciacca

Bumper stickers are suburban graffiti. "I Touch Eternity—I Teach" is especially sobering to me because I am a high school teacher. But you are a teacher too.

Curriculum plays a major role in education. The formal curriculum is the structured channel: lesson plans, lectures, exams, etc. Its essential medium is the spoken word, and its primary concern is the distribution of information.

The informal curriculum is not planned. It's spontaneous rather than structured, seen rather than heard. Often it is learned more subconsciously than consciously. The formal curriculum is what teachers teach. The informal curriculum is what teachers are. Jesus knew the incredible impact of the informal curriculum: "A student is not above his teacher, but everyone who is fully trained [formal] will be like his teacher [informal]" (Luke 6:40).

In our fathering, the informal curriculum is the most critical. What we teach in family devotions won't mean much if our life doesn't match what we say.

Several years ago the Lord allowed a personal failure in my fathering to prove this point. While on vacation our family spent a day in an amusement park. One of the rides had a height requirement that was a half-inch taller than my youngest son. When I saw the sadness on his face I thought, "This isn't fair—he's so close." So, I told him to stand on his toes when the man came to measure the questionable participants. Well, Geoff got caught. Later, the Lord spoke to me about the lesson I had really taught to my son that day: Disobedience is okay if you don't get caught. I apologized.

My formal curriculum to my four children has always been to respect authority. But my lifestyle, my informal instruction, had communicated in this instance that lying is really okay sometimes.

Our children will catch our inconsistencies. I have failed and sought forgiveness many times since that afternoon in the amusement park.

Dads, do you defy the law by misusing a company car or credit card? How often do you speed when police aren't around? (My kids ask me!) Do you lie to telephone callers? Make no mistake, the informal curriculum will be what's caught. You are not only being heard, you are being watched.

What's Dad Doing Home So Much?

Chuck Miller

I am a busy, overextended youth pastor. God has blessed me immensely. My ministry has multiplied manyfold. I am asked to speak at youth conventions across the country. I am writing books. My family and I have moved to a new city where I will be teaching, leading seminars, and spending more time at home. By any measure, I am at the top of my profession.

My eight-year-old son noticed that I am home more (although often too exhausted to move). He asked my wife why I was home so much. She explained that as a result of the move, I was going to be home more now, so that I could spend more time with him and his younger sister. My son was not pleased. His response pierced my soul. I saw that he did not desire to be in my presence. I had the recognition of my peers, but not of my son.

I was scared to death. I had spent fifteen years of my life in youth ministry and had watched teenagers who had grown apart from their parents. I had seen the impact of this on their lives. What am I going to do? I have a degree that tells me how to relate to youth and children. I have read books, even written some. And I am failing. I call on God: "Father, am I strong enough to give up the recognition of my peers? How can I save my family, my relationship with my son?" Suddenly I realize that when I stand before God, He will not ask me about my ministry. He will ask me first about my own life, next about my wife, and then about the children He has entrusted to me. Only then will He ask about my ministry.

As a family, we began to slip away on weekends. My wife suggested that our eight-year-old and I needed to go off alone. This did not set well with me. To do so meant that I had failed. It meant I had to repair a relationship. I had to admit that I was not Mr. Dad. But he and I went away. We played catch, rode bikes, and fixed food. We spent time together.

Through God, amazing things happened in our relationship between the time when my son was eight and when he was eighteen. As a senior in high school, he was co-captain of the soccer team. He was strong, handsome, funny, and well-known. One day, as we were walking through the only mall in our hometown, I suddenly felt the leather of his letterman's jacket as he put his arm around me. Oh, my. My teenage son with his arm around me in public. "Dad, I just want you to know that I love you, that I am so proud to have you as my dad." Everything I had given up ten years earlier could never have meant as much as the sound of those words. No applause, trophy, or title could gain the respect of my son. Just me.

"So that you, your children and their children after them may fear the Lord your God as long as you live" (Deuteronomy 6:2). Godly men think multi-generationally. Godly men stop and take inventory of the relational foundation between them and each child in their family. Godly men, empowered by God's Spirit, have the courage and wisdom to change schedules, vocabularies, and response patterns.

How are your children doing? Do they have hobbies and interests? Are you an active participant with them in their hobbies and interests? What's happening between you and each child in your family? Is there laughter? Do you invite them to pray for you about things in your life? Do they invite you to pray for things in their lives? Are you raising your children as human doers, or are you making time for them to become human beings? What might you be to each of your children this week? Pray God will give you hints and the power to do it.

Making Up for Lost Fathering Time

Ken R. Canfield

Whenever I go to a Kansas City Royals baseball game, I can't help noticing the kids in the stadium who have been "loaded down" by their fathers with enough baseball paraphernalia to open their own stand in the parking lot. The kid can't decide whether to wave his pennant, his inflatable baseball bat, or his giant foam "We're number one" hand. Not a vendor goes by without the father signaling, grabbing for his wallet, and buying the child peanuts, popcorn, Cokes, hot dogs.

The father is certainly being lavish, and no doubt the kid is grateful—but when it comes to consistency, you need to realize that these "blowouts" are part of a pendulum swing. A month of not hearing from their father and then *"pow."* Two weeks of scarcely seeing Dad around the house and then *"pow."* It can really shake a kid up.

Children need regular and predictable contact with their fathers. If you are away from your kids, a phone call once a week is more beneficial to their development than four trips to Disney World strewn haphazardly throughout the year.

Avoid the mentality of wanting to make up for lost time. I don't know what your situation is. Maybe you're disappointed at how you've fathered up to this point. Maybe you are divorced and living away from your kids. Whatever your situation, avoid the urge to try to make up for lost time. Don't throw wild extravaganzas for your child simply because you haven't expressed your love enough in the past.

6

The Promises You Make to Your Parents

Gary Smalley and John Trent

This was a difficult chapter to title. Although Genesis 2:24 says "a man shall leave his father and mother and be united to his wife," there is a sense in which a man never leaves his father and mother. This is true even of those who did not know their parents. We are products of their behavior and lifestyle. We share in their tragedies and their sickness. We are tied to them, often, long after their deaths.

But Genesis is correct, and though various ties linger, the relationship has changed, or at least should change. The following articles represent a sampling of promises to "deal with" the continuing negative influences with which our parents can still control us. Perhaps these articles will enable you to promise your parents that you'll deal with the past.

• Harold Bussell explores how it is possible to honor our parents even though we don't respect them.

• Ken Canfield explores how we often transfer our negative images of our fathers to God, and how we can avoid the mistake in the future.

• Dave Simmons tells us his own moving story of hatred for his dad and how he turned that into love. Then Dave goes on to tell us how he started to fall into the same mistakes his dad did—and how he finally broke the cycle.

• And finally, Gordon Dalbey tells us how God can be the Father we never knew.

Honoring Parents You Don't Respect

Harold L. Bussell

T here are many grown men who continually suffer from wounds inflicted by dysfunctional, abusive or non-loving parents. It is quite difficult for these men to seriously consider God's command in Exodus 20 to honor your parents, but the commandment is not just for children. If you remember, this command was first given to adults. To not understand this is to miss the ultimate reason for the commandment. The predominate group leaving Egypt were middle-aged people, people moving from slavery to freedom. But freedom from slavery never frees us from responsibility.

The Egyptians had used death to solve social problems—the deformed, the unwanted, and the elderly were often left to die in the desert. The Israelites had seen this. Because this was the model for the Jews who grew up in Egypt, they were vulnerable to reverting to this cultural practice when their wilderness journeys began. And the Jews faced excruciating difficulties traveling in the desert with the the elderly and infirm. God knew the elderly and infirm would be an added burden to them on their journey.

At some point we all face the added burdens that come with aging parents. They have failing bodies, often limited financial resources, added fears of the future and of death. Sometimes personality problems and sins of the past become intensified with aging and senility. If you have ever traveled with an elderly person you'll know the responsibilites and stress it entails. But despite whatever difficulties come with the age of your parents, "honoring thy father and mother" is a primary way God shows us that the family is the vehicle by which He has ordered human life, for the good of society.

The reason why we find this command difficult is that we confuse respect with honor. Respect is what people earn as a result of their character. Honor is a matter of the will. It is possible to honor and love those whom God has given us as parents, even though we don't respect them. The sixth commandment doesn't require us to respect them, it simply calls us to honor them for what they stand for.

As a parent, our role is to share our faith with our children. And one of the only ways to teach our children is by the way we honor our parents.

But old age does not have to mean infirmity of the character and soul of your parents. The Bible presents the mountain peak of life as old age. Why? Because character does not happen by attending a retreat or memorizing Bible verses. Character is the byproduct of a lifelong process. The elderly do have something to teach us. The elderly are untapped wells of insight, wisdom, and ministry.

My grandmother had a stroke when she was ninety-two years old. When I visited the home in which she was staying, I asked one of the nurses if she would read my future letters to my grandmother. In these letters I told her that she now had the precious gift of time that I did not have. I asked her to take on a ministry of prayer for the people I was working with. Until she died three years later, she had a significant ministry of prayerful intercession. Part of the honoring process is finding significant ministries for those facing added burdens of aging.

How we care for the burdens of the elderly verifies our world view. Christ, our Lord, modeled this on the Cross. In his very last breath he made provision for the care of his mother.

When Our Earthly Fathers Sour Us on the Heavenly Father

Ken R. Canfield

A friend of mine tells me of a theology class he took years ago in seminary, where on the first day of the semester, the professor handed out a personal questionnaire. Many of the questions on the survey had to do with the student's perceptions of his father and the relationship he had with him. The surveys were collected and no more was said of it. The students forgot all about them during the rigorous months of studying about the First Person of the Trinity, His attributes, His work, and His words. At the end of the course, the professor handed out a second survey. This time the students were supposed to honestly record their perceptions of God and feelings about their relationship with Him. The questions, in fact, were the same as on the first survey they took, but redirected toward the heavenly Father, not their earthly ones. When the professor returned both sets of surveys, including the previously forgotten one, the students were astounded that even after a whole semester of studying about God, they still had trouble differentiating Him relationally with their earthly dads.

Here's the trick. We need to understand that when God reveals Himself as father, He is not simply using "father" as a metaphor. It is not that He is like a father; He is a father, and He is your father. In a deep and very real sense, God is a father. In fact, notice in the Scriptures that when God does relate Himself to earthly fathers, it is to show how much beyond compare He is. For example, when Jesus says, "If you, then, though you are evil, know how to give good gifts to your children, how much more will your Father in heaven give good gifts to those who ask him!" (Matthew 7:11).

God is a father, and He is your father.

The benefit of this truth—the way it sets us free—is that we can let God reveal to us what type of father He is. We don't have to assume that He is an inconsistent, distant, authoritarian figure. We can let Him show us who He is: compassionate, consistent, inclined to our good. I have encouraged many men to pray this prayer: "Heavenly Father, show me what type of father You are." God will answer this prayer. And your map will never be the same again.

Father Power

Dave Simmons

"The principal danger to fatherhood today is that fathers do not have the vital sense of father power that they have had in the past. Because of a host of pressures from society, the father has lost the confidence that he is naturally important to his children—that he has the power to affect children, guide them, help them grow. He isn't confident that fatherhood is a basic part of being masculine and the legitimate focus of his life."—Dr. Henry Biller

We buried Dad, Major Amos E. Simmons (Ret.), in the family cemetery by a country road about one half-mile from where he was born and raised. The soldiers came from Ft. Polk, draped an American flag over his silver-blue casket, and saluted him with rifle fire. A solitary trooper played taps on his bugle. We prayed. I cried.

I cried because I had loved him for only three years. I had hated him for twenty-five years and had liked him for eight years. I felt cheated. I wanted my dad back. We were busy building good memories to replace the painful ones.

They were painful because he did not know much about fathering, and I did not know much about "sonning." It took me thirty-three years to mature enough to make the effort to understand Dad and start being a good son.

Dad had three goals: He wanted me to love him, to be hard-nosed and aggressive, and to be a high achiever. His heart was right. His intentions were okay. Unfortunately, his philosophy and methodology were a little suspect. From the moment I was born, he had me in a training program.

To make me tough, he would walk me out to the playground and actually pick fights for me. I remember once in Berlin, Germany Dad looked out the window and saw three German boys walking by our house. He ran over, threw open the door and said, "Get out there and whip those boys, and if you don't, I'm going to whip you."

To develop me into an outstanding achiever, he employed several techniques. A favorite was to set impossible goals. One time, while we were living in Ft. Riley, Kansas, I got a bicycle for Christmas. It came unassembled, and Dad said, "Son, you wanna ride it? Put it together." He gave me the parts, the tools, and the directions. I couldn't read yet, so I did the best I could by looking at the pictures. Shortly, I was hopelessly lost and started crying. He brusquely knocked me aside and said, "Get away, stupid, I knew you couldn't do it." His theory was that if I had such high goals, I could never accomplish them, and in frustration I would make even greater efforts to achieve. The key was to keep me on the leading edge of a high-intensity effort.

A variation of this technique was to nudge the goals higher if I started to get close. I didn't. I made several second-string All-American teams my junior year at Georgia Tech, and Dad wanted to know why I didn't make first team on every All-American team. The St. Louis Cardinals drafted me in the second round, and Dad wanted to know what it felt like to be only second. (Joe Namath was their first-round choice.) I played in three college All-Star games, was co-captain of the South team in the Senior Bowl, and was linebacker with Dick Butkus in the Chicago All-Star game, and Dad was curious as to why they interviewed him at halftime on national TV and not me.

Another ploy to make me successful was to goad me into a frenzied temper tantrum and, flying high on an adrenaline overdose, I could blast through any barrier to new heights. Just pitch a fit. Get mad. Go crazy. It didn't matter who or what I got mad at. The trick was to get me angry at myself, at him, or anything, and then redirect my fury toward my task.

I had three choices why I could feel like a failure: because I did not reach impossible goals; because the goals I did reach were not significant; or because I acted so silly in the process. In any case, I was bound to feel like a failure. I never experienced the feelings of success. I was in a lot of pain, and I associated this pain with my dad.

I seethed with bitterness and rebellion toward Dad. I could not confront him openly (I tried once and he broke my nose), so I struck back in sneaky ways that I couldn't get caught and punished for. I deliberately sabotaged things and failed at things just to watch him blow up. I withheld the only things Dad needed from me: love and respect. I never told him I loved or respected him, and I never asked for advice or went to him with a problem. I deprived him of all the rewards of fatherhood.

My greatest blow of revenge on Dad came when I chose where to play college football. I had scholarship offers from all over the nation, including his beloved LSU and West Point, either of which would have been his crowning reward for fatherhood. I decided to play for coach Bobby Dodd at Georgia Tech because it was 1,500 miles from him. I had to get away from him. I didn't want him to ever see me play another ball game. He saw only three of my college games in four years. This racked his soul.

But I didn't leave Dad behind when I left home, and he didn't leave me behind when he died. Our fathers never leave us. They hang around in our minds for the rest of our lives, and their voices keep repeating all the things we heard as we grew up.

To this day, I can't capture the feeling of a job well done. I constantly focus on my mistakes and am negative toward all that I do. I set goals too high and fail. I sabotage things and fail. I get angry and emotional and I fail. I resent and rebel against authority and fail. I go to ridiculous lengths to reach perfection in order to get compliments and recognition for my work, but then I can't accept appreciation and feel like a failure. I carry the voice of Major Amos E. Simmons, the Commander, in my heart. He speaks to me through my emotions and I still believe everything he told me. Even though all facts say I am successful, my emotions convince me that I am a failure. My dad still exercises formidable power in my life.

Nothing is more powerful in a person's life than a father. Father power can be positive or negative; it can make the difference between success and failure. Negative father power left me twisted and bent. Not only did it disable me, but I saw the same destructive father power flowing from me to my children. "Ole man" John gave it to "ole man" Luther, who passed it on to Amos, who deposited it in me, and I am determined to stop the flow. The cycle must be broken.

I realized I needed to convert *de*structive father power into *con*structive father power. To start this conversion process, I had to deal with Dad. With a supporting wife and some professional counseling, I recognized my own share of the fault and took responsibility for it. It wasn't until I was thirty-three years old that I finally matured enough to understand Dad and realize that Dad did love me. No father ever loved a son more. He was proud of me, amazed even, and no one wanted to have a son love him back as much as he did. He simply did not know how to express his love and pride. He was severely handicapped: no mother, childhood lumberjack, battlefield trauma, army life, and his dad chopped up cars and abused him. All he knew about fathering had been passed down through the Simmons' bloodline. The cycle at work.

I saw that Dad hated his imperfections and mistakes more than I did. He was a prisoner trapped behind his own personality and didn't know how to break out. He wanted to break the cycle too. And he tried. He just never learned how. He did not know how to be a family shepherd and transfer positive father power.

If we were ever to salvage our relationship, I had to take the initiative. I experimented with different techniques on love and discovered some amazingly successful principles, that I can't go into now but that I share through my books and seminars. As a result of these secret love techniques, Dad and I inaugurated a great love relationship that thrived until his death.

Our love grew. I looked forward to going home. I would drive up, honk the horn, get out of the car, and Dad would come out, grab me in a smothering bear hug and lift me right off the ground. He would tell me how good it was to see me and say, "Son, I sure love you and am proud of you."

We were breaking the cycle. And I am convinced that if you do not repair your paternal cords, you will never be fully released to give your own children all that you could. The first step in providing my children with positive, constructive father power was to get things right with my dad. Only then could I begin to be a balanced family shepherd.

I wish I could tell you that it has been easy for me and that overnight I experienced startling success simply by willing it. But in my life, the pendulum makes wide swings: I win lopsided victories and lose with great flourish.

Take my son Brandon, for instance. Brandon went out for basketball in the eighth grade and made the team. I went bananas. My boy! Playing ball! Big game tonight! I showed up thirty minutes before warm-ups and staked out a section for me and my photography equipment. I scouted the gym to locate the best camera angles, erected my tripod, arranged my telephoto lenses, and started drawing up my rebound charts and shot charts.

I took some magnificent photos during warm-ups. Luckily, I was also able to slip the coach a few last minute strategy ideas before the tip-off. It was loads of fun being a typical father in the stands.

The game started, and it didn't take long before I put down my cameras. I folded my tripod and forgot about the rebound and shot charts. I got depressed and angry. Brandon was a spectacular flop.

Oh, he got lots of rebounds and points, but it was evident that he was out there fooling around trying to have fun. He acted as if it were a sport or recreational game. He didn't crash to the boards for rebounds. He never once dived for a loose ball. He loped around impervious to fast breaks, filling lanes, and following shots. I was mortified. Humiliated! He acted as if he didn't know he had to go out and win and take a shot at the record books. He was my son. He was representing me out there.

I could not wait to get him in the car after the game. With my wife Sandy, sitting quietly in the front seat, I yelled at him all the way home, "Where is your pride, boy? Don't you care? You didn't hustle. You didn't try. You were terrible. I'll tell you what: I don't care what your coach says, what you say, or what the other players say—you are off the team if I ever again catch you not giving it all you've got. Either you hustle or you quit."

We drove up our driveway, and when I got out, I saw Brandon sitting in the backseat, quietly crying. I walked up the stairs, opened the door, and stepped back to let my wife in. As she walked by, she shot me a smoldering glance and said one word— a thunderbolt word that electrified my heart . . . "Amos!"

My mouth fell open with a shock. I couldn't believe it. She was right. After all those years with my dad harping on me about sports, I was doing the same thing to my son, and I knew better and had sworn that I would never do to my son what my dad did to me. I was just like Amos. Destructive father power bleeds through generation after generation. All I had to do to fail was relax and do what came naturally. It takes commitment and exertion over the long haul to convert father power to an asset. We have enough 100-yard-dash dads: we need more cross-country fathers. The cycle must be broken.

Later we moved to Little Rock and Brandon tried out for the junior high football team. He made it! But he came home and made the tragic announcement that he was a quarterback. This was terrible news. As an old linebacker, I hate quarterbacks.

Anyway, the kid had an arm. He could fire the ball.

The season started, and he came out passing. He did great. He moved the team right down the field, and I was proud. That was my boy out there.

About the fourth game, however, he broke down and went to pieces. He played terrible. He fumbled the snap several times; he tossed a couple of pitchouts over the halfback's head and effortlessly completed interceptions. He single-handedly lost the game for us.

In the stands, I began to get embarrassed. Then disgusted. Finally, I got so angry that, at halftime, I sat back, folded my arms across my chest, and started getting psyched up.

Then, all of a sudden, I realized what was happening. I stopped and thought of Major Amos. I thought of myself and the fourth generation rule. I remembered I wanted to break the cycle and not do what was so natural for me to do. So, I prayed.

During the second half, Brandon played no better. But I deliberately concentrated on my attitude and emotions. I forced myself to withdraw emotionally from the game. I backed out of the contest and prevented myself from getting psyched up. I prepared myself for my meeting with Brandon after the game.

The game was a lopsided catastrophe. Sandy, Helen, and I waited in the car for Brandon to come out of the locker room. The car was blanketed in silence. Brandon eventually shuffled out and climbed into the backseat.

We drove homeward and eventually came to our street. I asked the girls if they wanted to go home or, as was our custom, drive on into Little Rock and get some frozen yogurt. Since they wanted to go home, I wheeled up our driveway and dropped them off.

Brandon and I drove to town, parked, walked into the store, got our frozen yogurt and sat down. Not a word had passed. When we were almost done, Brandon put down his spoon, looked searchingly at me, and asked, "Dad, why are you doing this?"

I said, "Well, Son, I'll tell ya. I just want you to know that I love you and accept you totally. Just as you are. I love you whether you're the football hero or whether you play terrible. I love you because you're Brandon and not because you're number ten on the football squad."

Brandon's face lit up, and he burst out with all kinds of comments about the game. He eventually got around to the big question: "Come on Dad. Tell me. What did you really think of the game? Tell me how you really think I did."

Fantastic, I thought. Now, he's really asking for it. I can blast him now! But I didn't. I paused and asked him, "Well, Brandon, what do you think? How did you play?"

And he proceeded to tell me exactly how he did. He listed every mistake and explained how he made it and what he needed to do to correct it. He understood it all.

Men, we don't need to follow our kids around pointing out every mistake or informing them of all their shortcomings. They know. They are quite aware. They need a family shepherd dedicated to building them up and encouraging them. One who believes in them and will bring out the best in them.

Later, as we drove home, Brandon's spirits soared, and he got carried away. Before I knew it, he said something that I will never forget. It was the highest compliment I have ever received.

"Dad, you know what I wish?" he asked. "I wish you and me could be on the same team. Wouldn't it be great if, on offense, I could be quarterback, and you could be the tight end, and, on defense, we could both be linebackers together? Dad, I wish we could play on the same high school team, then play at Georgia Tech together and go on and play for the Dallas Cowboys. Dad, I sure wish we could play on the same team."

After a long pause, Brandon must have thought he might have offended me because he rushed in with this consoling disclaimer: "But, Dad, even if we were brothers, I would still want you for a dad!"

He wanted us to play on the same team. I think back to August of 1961, when a young man left El Paso, Texas by train and traveled all the way to Georgia Tech in Atlanta to get as far away from his dad as possible to play college football. He didn't want his dad in the same state during a football game! Now comes Brandon one generation later, and he wants his dad in the same huddle.

Father power. Father power can be negative or positive. Who and what you are will be stamped into your children and will be passed down through the generations, to the second, third, and fourth generations.

Men, I proclaim to you that the cycle can be broken. You can stop a negative legacy and initiate a positive legacy. The cycle can be broken.

A Father to the Fatherless

Gordon Dalbey

Clearly, the Scriptures describe God as having all the characteristics of the father needed by the son. At various times, some of these may come to him through his earthly father. But when they do not, he need not despair; he need only go to his heavenly Father.

In praying with men I have seen God minister His Father-love in a variety of ways. Sometimes, a man received no love at all from his earthly father, who perhaps abandoned the mother at his birth or died early. I have simply laid hands on that man and prayed for the love of the Father to be poured out upon him, inviting the man himself to ask for the Father's love, too, as a gesture of opening his heart to receive it. Often in such cases, the man may say, "I feel warm all over," or, "a peace kind of came over me." Again, he may receive a vision of himself as a little boy climbing onto Jesus' lap and being held.

I sometimes encourage a man to write down a list of things he wishes his earthly father had given him, and then offer that list to the Father God. One man's father had played semi-pro baseball but never had taught his son to play. As a boy, the man had felt as if his father were judging him as inadequate or "a klutz," so he stayed away from sports even though he longed to participate. "Do you think the Father God can teach me how to play baseball?" he asked, not without skepticism. Stepping out in faith, I assured him that God could do that and urged him to pray accordingly. I confess a fear and doubt in my heart at the time. Yet, within a week, this man went to a Christian men's gathering and struck up a conversation with another man. As they chatted, both sensed a budding friendship. And then, as they were parting and exchanging business cards, the other man mentioned that he played softball in a local church league—in fact he had once coached baseball—and asked if the man might want to play on the softball team.

Another man's life was a litany of troubles with women, and he declared, "My dad never taught me a thing about women. Do you think the Father God can teach me about women?" I assured him that God could show him exactly what he needed to know about women in order to bring his relationships with them into harmony with God's plan. When he prayed, he asked the Father God simply, "Please teach me about women like my father never did." I prayed quietly in the Spirit, and moments later he reported a clear "sense" of several ways he could change his responses to women. "I guess I've been pretty rational and cut-and-dried about things, and women see things more in terms of relationships and feelings," he said. "Maybe I can begin to listen a little better to my girlfriend's feelings instead of always trying to solve every problem outright by analyzing it."

Several men have said that their fathers never called them out to be with other men, and when we asked the Father God to fill that void, He replied in different ways according to each man's deeper need. One man received phone calls from two other men shortly afterward; another man began to think of men he could call, and did so, thanking God.

To reach such a point of crying out for the Father God's help, a man must have been sufficiently disappointed in other persons. Many men are trapped in such a limbo of disappointment, however, and do not realize that the way out is not to give up all hope and withdraw, but rather, to confess their misplaced hope in other human beings and begin to place it instead in the Father God.

When a man realizes he has gone to other persons for something only God can give, he may want very much to release his spouse, children, parents, and all others from the terrible burden of giving him complete love. He may want at last to go to the Source. But, having lived so long in the world, he very likely does not know how.

We men have been shopping for milk so long at the store that we have forgotten the way back to the farm. That is, we are so accustomed to seeking love from other persons that we do not know how to approach the Father God for it.

Agnes Sanford used to say that Jesus is like a step-down transformer because He renders the immeasurable power of God personally available to us.

So I urge men to draw closer to the Father God by getting to know Jesus. But I warn them that doing so ultimately brings them to the Cross, which means death to the human self. To draw close to the Father through Jesus requires that a man give up all hope of ever receiving the love he needs from another human being. It means sacrificing at last the idols you have made of your "loved ones," and releasing those persons and those relationships to the Father for His cleansing and renewal.

7

The Promises You Make to Your Friends

Gary Smalley and John Trent

The story is told of the British poet Lord Byron as a schoolboy, when he ran to intervene during a beating a bully was giving one of Byron's friends. Byron bravely asked how many stripes the bully was planning to inflict on his friend. "What's that to you?" thundered the bully. "Because, if you please," replied Byron, trembling with rage and fear, "I would take half."

We men dream of friendships like that, but we seldom have them. But the Bible tells us friendships are important. It tells of the loyalty and sacrifice of Jonathan for David, of close family friendships like Ruth, Orpah, and Naomi, or Esther and Mordecai. We read of the apostles' devotion to one another through Jesus' leadership of their little band. And Jesus Himself is our primary model of sacrifice for one another. Paul's relationship with Timothy reflects devotion, encouragement, accountability, prayer, and affirmation.

I (Gary) attended a dinner with Charles Colson which was given by Prison Fellowship for inmates being released from prison, and their wives. I'll never forget Chuck's words to those men as they were reentering society: "You'll go back to prison unless you have the power of God on your side . . . and a friend."

Such is the power of friendship—something indispensable for all men who desire to be promise keepers. Accountability, loyalty, sacrifice. As you read more about friendship in this section, ask yourself, "Am I only looking for friends, or am I seeking to *be* a friend?"

Spiritual Fellowship

Jerry Bridges

Encourage one another daily, as long as it is called today, so that none of you may be hardened by sin's deceitfulness. (Hebrews 3:13)

One day I received an urgent phone call from a friend asking if we could meet. We get together periodically over lunch or breakfast to share what God is doing in our lives, to encourage and counsel one another, and to share prayer requests. I'm not discipling him, nor is he discipling me. We're both involved in ministering to others, but we need and appreciate the mutual strengthening that comes from these times together.

That day, however, wasn't just an ordinary time. My friend was hurting. Over lunch he poured out his heart to me concerning some difficult problems he was facing at work. I listened, offered a suggestion or two from the Bible of how he should respond, and committed myself to pray for him. As I drove back to my office, I did pray for him; and when I arrived home that evening, I jotted down his need on my "emergency" prayer list.

His situation did not improve suddenly and dramatically, but over a period of several months God answered our prayers. During that time I continued to encourage him, to pray for him, and to explore various alternatives with him until we saw God work.

This incident illustrates the importance and vital necessity of spiritual fellowship, or what I call "communion" with one another. God has created us to be dependent both on Him and on one another. His judgment that "it is not good for the man to be alone" (Genesis 2:18) is a principle that speaks not only to the marriage relationship but also to the necessity of spiritual fellowship among all believers. None of us has the spiritual wherewithal to "go it alone" in the Christian life.

Spiritual fellowship is not a luxury but a necessity, vital to our spiritual growth and health. We have seen that biblical fellowship involves both a sharing of our common life in Christ and a sharing with one another what God has given to us. One of the most important things we can share with one another is the spiritual truth that God has been teaching us, which might be of great help to fellow believers.

J. I. Packer made this insight about this type of fellowship:

God made us in such a way that our fellowship with himself is fed by our fellowship with Christians, and requires to be so fed constantly for its own deepening and enrichment.

Scripture contains a number of exhortations and examples on this subject. For example, Solomon says in Proverbs 27:17, "As iron sharpens iron, so one man sharpens another." It is in the exchange with each other of what God is teaching us that our minds and hearts are whetted and stimulated. We learn from one another as together we learn from God.

Another advantage of fellowship is the mutual admonishing or encouraging of each other during temptation or an attack of Satan.

Hebrews 3:13 says, "Encourage one another daily, as long as it is called Today, so that none of you may be hardened by sin's deceitfulness." Then in 10:24-25, "Let us consider how we may spur one another on toward love and good deeds. Let us not give up meeting together, as some are in the habit of doing, but let us encourage one another—and all the more as you see the Day approaching." Note the emphasis on encouraging one another in the face of temptation, and spurring one another on toward love and good deeds. To be kept from temptation and to be stimulated when our zeal for Christian duty is flagging, we need both the public teaching of our pastors and the mutual encouragement and admonishing of one another. The latter seems to be the main thrust of Hebrews 10:24-25.

Acceptance at What Price?

Ken Abraham

Each of us wants to be accepted by our peers. That desire is not unique to teenagers, nor does it lessen with age. Unfortunately, most of us are only too quick to compromise our values and beliefs to gain approval of "the crowd."

In his book, *Darryl* (Bantam, 1992), All-Star baseball player Darryl Strawberry describes how early in his career he got sucked into this trap by becoming part of a group of guys on the New York Mets who called themselves "the scum bunch." The scum bunch was a group of grown men who sat in the back of the players' bus or the team plane; they drank too much beer, blasted their music, and threw food around.

Says Strawberry, "I fell into this group partly because I felt that they had kind of a license to be bad. I know now that it was a mistake because I let the group have too much influence over me. If the scum bunch said throw that hamburger out the window or spit beer on someone, then I'd do it with a vengeance because I wanted to belong."

Most of us have experienced something similar. Years ago, shortly after becoming a Christian, I went out with some of my buddies for our usual "Friday Night Mayhem." This was back in the days when we foolishly believed that alcohol and gasoline were a safe mixture. As soon as I piled into the car along with the other guys, one of my friends offered me a beer.

"No thanks, man. I don't drink anymore. I'm a Christian now."

"Come on, Ken. What's one drink going to hurt? God's not going to send you to hell for taking one drink, is He?"

"Well, no. I don't think so," I replied. I relented and took the beer, self-righteously announcing as I chugged a big swig, "Okay, but only this one."

"Sure, sure," one of my buddies replied. "Who cares?" In their minds, the point had been proven. For all my "Jesus talk," no real transformation had taken place in my life. I was still "one of the guys." That one beer was the equalizer, our common denominator.

I learned a tough lesson that night, perhaps the same one that Darryl Strawberry learned the hard way, too: "If you have to compromise your values in order to be accepted, you haven't won a thing, but you've lost a lot."

I'm Blessed, Tired, and Alone

Chuck Miller

I f you viewed the ministry with which I'm involved from a business context, in one year we've seen a tenfold increase in market impact. That's exciting, but I'm tired. There seem to be so
many demands on my life because of this growth. I feel alone. Yes,
I have a wonderful wife who is very supportive, but there are no
men my age supporting me. When I read Exodus 17, I watch a
team of men fight the Amalekites. As Moses takes the staff of God
and holds his hands heavenward, the Israelites are on the offensive.
When Moses gets tired and has to lower his hands the Amalekites
go on the offensive. Aaron perceives how tired Moses is and slips a
stone under him and he sits down. Aaron then holds up one arm
while Hur holds up the other. Joshua overcomes the Amalekite
army.

*God, I need some Aarons and Hurs in my life. I need men to join
me.*

I observe men in a large congregation. I identify seven. I ask
the senior pastor if he feels these men could be Aaron and Hur to
me. He says yes, but makes the comment that each one is so busy,
he would be surprised if they would do it. I ask them to gather
in our home, just for a time when I could share my heart with
them. I tell them I am in need of men to support my life and to
hold me accountable. We gather. We study Ephesians 2:19-22
together. We talk about our lives. Then I ask if they would be willing to come alongside me, to pray for me, to cheer for me, to hold
me accountable, to be Aaron and Hur to me. We could also be
that to one another. Each one accepts.

Since then, we've gathered every other week for three years. We laugh, we share hurts. I remember the morning a normally happy person arrived looking like death warmed over. When we asked him what was happening, he said, "Well, in this time of recession suddenly banks are calling loans due. I meet with a bank at 9:30 this morning. Before this day is over I may have to declare bankruptcy." That was a heavy morning. We prayed him through a dark time in his life.

Another morning one man arrived looking haggard. As brothers we felt that he needed to get away with his wife to laugh and relax. The pressures of work were too much. It was fun when we said, "Well, we'll ask your wife Sunday where you're going next weekend."

We are growing closer to each other. I need them. They give me insight, they correct me, they bother me. They are Aaron and Hur to me. It's wonderful to defeat the "Amalekites" of your life with teams of godly men.

How to Be a Man of Integrity

William Gaultiere

As a psychologist I meet men of all ages with a variety of problems, but one thing almost all of them have in common is that they are searching for integrity. They are consulting me because they need a mirror in which to see their soul. They need to take an honest and sincere look at who they are and what their lives are like. This means things like getting in touch with their feelings, admitting they have needs, acknowledging their shortcomings, learning from past mistakes, and repairing the emotional damage in their lives.

Integrity is a difficult attribute to develop. Many of the men whom I meet outside of my office have very little integrity and seem to make no effort to change. These men without integrity live an unexamined life: they're not aware of most of what they feel, they don't admit to their faults, they don't learn from past mistakes. When they have a problem in life they avoid taking responsibility for it by blaming and criticizing other people. They have no one whom they actively rely on to hold them accountable to live rightly. In fact, they hide their true selves from others, and when they are confronted about one of their weaknesses they become defensive and evasive.

Integrity was a weakness in my own character until I began to implement into my life two things that I now regularly rely on. First, I seek honest feedback about me and my life from certain friends I trust. I share my feelings, my problems, my decisions, my life, my self with these people. And I ask questions like, "What do you think about how I handled this situation?" "How do you experience me in our relationship?" "What areas do I need to grow in?" "How can I be a better friend to you?"

The second thing I do is try to stop myself whenever I'm critical or judgmental of other people. Then I look in the mirror and ask myself, "Why am I angry at this person? Why am I being so hard on them?" More often than not I discover that I've been trying to take a speck out of my neighbor's eye when I have a log in my own eye! Either I am seeing in someone else an attribute or behavior of mine that I don't like, or I am seeing in this other person a characteristic that reminds me of ways I have been hurt in the past by people I trusted.

For instance, the other morning I was driving during rush hour in the slow lane of the freeway. I was a few generous car lengths behind the car in front me and was peacefully listening to my classical music station. Suddenly, a driver from the center lane swerved in front of my car, narrowly missing my front bumper, passed a car on my left, then swerved back into the center lane, and sped off into the distance. I gripped my steering wheel tightly and clenched my teeth in anger, as I screamed silently, "How rude! Doesn't he have any consideration for how I might have felt?"

Then I stopped and looked at myself. "I'm angry at him because I can be rude at times too, and I don't like that part of me. In fact, I try to overcompensate by being super-sensitive to others' feelings, and it becomes burdensome to me. Furthermore, I'm angry at that driver because he reminds me of how certain people have hurt me by not being sensitive to my needs."

Ouch! It hurts to look at yourself in the mirrors of how others see you and how you view others! But then, no price is too great to pay to be a man of integrity.

Strive to fulfill this promise to be a man of integrity and every other promise that makes a man will be attainable.

Grooming Your Pallbearers

Tim Kimmel

My wife, Darcy, and I were on a date, sitting in the corner of the restaurant waiting for our food. I took out my pen and started to mark lines on a paper napkin. When I was done, I had made an acceptable likeness of a casket.

I slid it across the table.

Darcy peeked at it, then rolled her eyes. She knew I hadn't been taking this milestone (the big forty) in my life as well as I should. But this time she had read my thinking wrong.

"How many people does it take to carry one of these?"

She looked at me with whimsical eyes that said, "What is he up to now?" but she gave the right answer. "Six."

"Darcy, if I died tomorrow, who would you ask to carry my casket?" I had plenty of friends who I believed would be willing to help with this task, assuming there was nothing more pressing in their appointment book. But I didn't want those types of people carrying me to my grave. I wanted people who would drop whatever they were doing in order to drop me. Our conversation reminded me I had some work to do in the area of committed friends.

I realize this could sound morbid, but I decided I needed to start grooming my pallbearers. Certainly not because I planned on needing them anytime soon. But they represent the people who have been with you through the best and the worst of times. It was obvious to me that if I wanted to have rich friendships I would have to be a loyal friend.

The problem is that our hurried and complicated lives make

grooming our pallbearers difficult. But friends are essential, and we teach our children well by demonstrating how valuable they are. Friendship brings with it untold hassles and inconveniences. Our children need to see us courageously enduring the frustration that goes with being a friend. When they see the rewards that come from consistently loving, they'll know the frustrations are worth it.

Why Beer Commercials Make Some Men Feel So Good

Robert Hicks

For men, even our friendships do not come easy. They are complicated, rarely evaluated, and never talked about. In the final analysis, once we marry and have kids, if friendships don't happen with the people we work with, they probably will never happen at all. But our need for friends or our need to romanticize about friends is a common yearning. Men dream of having friends like the ones on the beer ads. There we are drinking together after the rugged soccer or softball game, reliving the game, and enjoying one another's company.

But are the TV portrayals of men watering at their favorite pub true portraits of reality? Probably not. But if they are fantasies, why do they sell so well? A New York psychiatrist suggests, "You've seen those beer commercials. . . . That's not the way men are together or ever were, but it's the way they think they were and that's all that matters. Two men may be sitting at a bar and saying one word every ten minutes, but in their minds they're in one of those beer commercials" (Naifeh and Smith, *Why Can't Men Open Up?*, page 62).

Men are torn between two extremes. On one extreme are the many mythologies of friendship as seen in the tight bonds of Huck Finn and Tom Sawyer, Tonto and the Lone Ranger, Butch Cassidy and the Sundance Kid, or the Dukes of Hazzard. On the other extreme are the distant, cordial but cold relationships so common between men. How many of us have actually seen close male-to-male friendships? Our fathers were not known for them, and what about our grandfathers? At the same time I must ask myself, What am I modeling to my son? Does he see me as a friend to any other man? I hope he has and will continue to do so, but I fear I send him confusing messages. My son has asked me on several occasions in the past few years, "Dad, who is your best friend?" Why do I feel I am lying when I mention a name? I somehow know the connection he is making in his unsophisticated brain: "If he is Dad's best friend, why does Dad never spend any time with him?" Ouch! It's hard to value another man for no other reason than that you enjoy being with him. The list of men I really feel comfortable around and enjoy being with is very short.

Many men place no priority on forming male-to-male relationships. There is no way I can convince these men that friendship is important. I cannot make men feel what they do not feel or what they do not want to feel. But I do know that I have tasted a small sample of what the friendship magic is all about. It's the three-hour lunch where the waitress finally hands you the dinner menu. It's your friend stepping into your office at 2:00 p.m. and saying, "Let's get out of here and take in a movie." It's laughing at a funny magazine at 11:00 p.m. until you think your sides will split. It's having to tell your best friend that his wife has cancer because she doesn't have the courage to tell him. It's listening to a brother who confesses he just doesn't know how to make his wife happy. It's hearing the heart-rending confession of your friend's affair when you love both him and his wife. It's being there when a man's daughter dies or when he goes to court or when he goes Home to his Maker.

We can hide in the closets of competition, use emotional walls to protect us, or flee from the reality of our deepest fears, but when we do, we flee from our own manhood. The close, nonsexual presence of other men will affirm our manhood more than anything else. Through these encounters, we validate our experiences as men, lose our deep-seated dependence on women, and find the same-gender counterpart we need who truly understands what it is like to be a man. Dr. Ken Druck notes, "Having established ourselves as a man among men, we build confidence and free ourselves to trust others in close relationships."

The Authentic Friend

Edwin Louis Cole

I found Brad in his motel room. After our initial greeting and embrace, we settled into chairs and he began repeating, "It's been unbelievable."

Years before, Brad stood to make his commitment to Christ. He became a friend, helped support the ministry, and he and his wife became friends with our staff. Now alone, in the midst of a divorce, far from his home, he and I sat in the privacy of his motel room, and I listened to his tearfully told story.

Brad had a trusted partner who carried on his business on a daily basis. But this formerly dependable individual did something Brad considered immoral and seditious. When confronted by Brad, he refused to acknowledge wrong, rebelled, and had to be fired.

The fired partner then went to work for someone else, took most of Brad's business with him, and left Brad mentally confused, emotionally crushed, and spiritually debilitated. When the pressure of it reached into Brad's home, his wife did not respond as he thought she should. Overwhelmed, he "opted out." His wife later verified that she had been selfishly disposed, didn't support him, and now wished she could do it all over. Weeping as she spoke of her estranged husband, she pleaded, "Please, Ed, do what you can."

There was little I could do in that lonely motel room. The best thing to do, I thought, was pray with him and be his friend. I put my hand on his shoulder and said, "Brad, I want to be a friend and help you all I can."

Instead of accepting my gesture, he looked up at me and said

sharply, "I've heard that before!" He paused, then asked, "\
a friend? Does anyone know how to be a friend? The men I t
said they were my friends, but they weren't." His remarks
sick sense in my gut, like a ten-ton sledgehammer had hit m

Faithful friends are life's greatest treasure. The unfaithful
Brad discovered, are life's greatest hurt. Being a true friend is one
the marks of a real man.

Availability

Bob Beltz

Bo was a successful young businessman when we met. We teamed up to develop a ministry to non-churched businessmen and their families. For over ten years now, Bo and I have had the pleasure of speaking at men's retreats around the country.

In the early days of our friendship, Bo used to say, "Everything I have is yours, except my wife." He meant it. If my car broke down, Bo considered it to be his problem. When I couldn't find a publisher for my first book, Bo put up the money to publish it and together we became Full Court Press.

When Allison and I were going through marital struggles Bo called every day and encouraged me to hang in there. When the idea for Cherry Hills Community Church seemed to be a leading from God, Bo put every ounce of his energy, creativity, ability, and resources into making the church a reality.

Bo taught me and modeled for me the promise of availability. Over the years I've had the opportunity to reciprocate in small ways. When the economy of Denver went into a tailspin Bo lost virtually everything. On several occasions Allison and I have made our resources available to help Bo make it through the tough times. Friendship begins to get very gutsy at these levels.

When my son was in surgery, Bo was there. When his wife, Gari, was in surgery, I was there. That's what authentic friendship looks like. It requires a commitment of availability of time, energy, and resources. Few friendships develop this level of commitment.

8

The Promises You Make to Worship and Fellowship

Gary Smalley and John Trent

Recently, a woman grabbed my arm after I had finished speaking at a conference on the enormous need we all have for affirmation.

"Dr. Trent, can I tell you my story?" she asked. "Actually, it's a story of something my son did with my granddaughter that illustrates what you've been talking about."

"My son has two daughters: one who's five, and one who is in the 'terrible twos.' For several years, he's taken the oldest girl out for a 'date' time, but it wasn't until recently that he'd asked the two-year-old out.

"On their first 'date,' he took her to breakfast at a fast-food restaurant. They'd just gotten their pancakes, when he decided it would be a good time to tell her how much he loved and appreciated her.

"'Jenny,' he said, 'I want you to know how much I love you and how special you are to Mom and me. We prayed for you for years, and now that you're here and growing up to be such a wonderful girl, we couldn't be more proud of you.'

"Once he said all this, he stopped talking and reached over for his fork to begin eating, but he never got the fork into his mouth.

"Jenny reached out and laid her little hand on her father's. His eyes went to hers, and in a soft, pleading voice she said, 'Longer, Daddy . . . longer.'

"He put his fork down and told her even more reasons why he and my daughter-in-law loved her. 'You're very kind, nice to your sister, full of energy. . . .' Then, he again reached for his fork only to hear the same words again. A second time . . . and a third . . . and a fourth time . . . and each time he heard the words, 'Longer, Daddy, longer.'"

That father never did get much to eat that morning, but his daughter feasted on words every child longs to hear. His words made such an impression on little Jenny, that a few days later she spontaneously ran up to her mother, jumped in her arms, and said, "I'm a really awesome daughter, Mommy. Daddy told me so!"

Words indeed have the awesome power to build us up or tear us down emotionally. This is particularly true within our families. Many people can clearly remember words of praise their parents spoke decades ago. Loving, supportive words that helped mold and shape their lives in significant ways. Sadly, other people remember only negative, cutting words—ones that have had an equal, but tragically opposite effect.

This is also true for affirmation in the church. Affirming words are like parental light switches. When people hear them, a whole room full of possibilities appears of what they can do and who they can become. "You're so fun to have around." "What a beautiful picture. You have such a good eye for color!" "What a great help you've been." Those are all examples of the kinds of comments that can make enormous differences in the quality of the lives of children and adults.

A couple of hours. A casual remark or two. Yet, great objects can be moved by small levers. Long years can be warmed or chilled by the lever of small happenings, small comments, and small encounters.

That lever lies in our hand . . . *in your hand*. The awesome potential of affirmation lies in your grasp.

The apostle Paul said it best: "Do not let any unwholesome talk come out of your mouths, but only what is helpful for building others up according to their needs" (Ephesians 4:29).

Commitment and Accountability

Jerry White

As iron sharpens iron, so one man sharpens another.
(Proverbs 27:17)

Two are better than one because they have a good return for their labor. For if either of them falls, the one will lift up his companion. But woe to the one who falls when there is not another to lift him up.
(Ecclesiastes 4:9-10, NASB)

The glamorized American West produced the image of the macho man. He is a loner—fiercely independent. He is tough, strong, handsome. The capable, independent woman is his female counterpart. Cigarette and liquor ads paint them indelibly in our minds as accountable to no one—totally self-sufficient.

Nothing could be further from the truth. Centuries of human history show that life demands accountability. Few people naturally do what is best for others. In the primitive or frontier past, natural elements held a person accountable to build shelter, gather food, and protect his family. In crowded industrial society, time clocks, pay clerks, foremen, and supervisors enforce accountability. The perverse nature of man tends to sloth, not diligence.

Even our sincere spiritual commitments, privately held, often go silently unfulfilled. And so we become discouraged—even a bit cynical—and hesitate to make new ones.

The only way I know to break this vicious cycle and keep our commitments is to make ourselves accountable to another person or group. Accountability is foundational to the New Testament concept of fellowship. But it rarely exists in the church body today. We have emaciated the meaning of fellowship in our efforts to make Christianity more appealing and acceptable to a sophisticated world.

Biblical fellowship cannot exist without "stimulating one another to love and good deeds," and "seeing that no one comes short of the grace of God" (Hebrews 10:24-25, 12:15, NASB). "Those who continue in sin, rebuke in the presence of all," and "bear one another's burdens." (1 Timothy 5:20, Galatians 6:2, NASB).

We need accountability for our personal lives, our ministries, and our families. Of the three, personal-life accountability is most crucial, since the latter two are more visible. Personal life could include such things as quiet time, prayer, Scripture memory, Bible study, a sin or habit we are trying to conquer, exercise, witnessing—or any other areas of personal need God brings to mind.

It would be ludicrous to have someone hold us accountable in twenty areas of our personal life. It would be like running through a preflight checklist in an airplane—necessary, but boring. Pick one or two areas of special need. Keep track of the other areas yourself. The act of accountable discipline in one area surprisingly spills over into other areas of life.

For example, suppose you had made a commitment to have a fifteen-minute daily quiet time, reading the Bible and praying. Ask a friend to check with you weekly on the specifics. How many quiet times did you have and for how long? Don't let him be easy on you by saying, "Well, how did it go this week?" And don't give a noncommittal response such as, "Well, I did okay, but I could do better." Be specific.

To whom should we make ourselves accountable? I would like to say the church. But it won't work. By the time the church as a body becomes aware of personal needs, it is most often too late. Accountability needs to be to a person—your spouse or a close friend.

Accountability also can occur in a small group. Such accountability can be very effective for everyone involved. Two are better than one. One person does sharpen the life of another. If your commitments are sincere, why not make them real by adding accountability to the commitment as insurance?

Accountability puts teeth into commitment. And it forces you to open up an area of your life to scrutiny by another. Not everyone is willing to do that—to take the risk of revealing the inner life. In doing so, we are not as independent and self-sufficient. Accountability puts pressure on us to perform and opens the door to failure. But the rewards fully outweigh the risks. Consider the great sense of accomplishment as spiritual commitments become reality.

Bringing Out the Best

Andrew T. LePeau

We can make a major contribution to the life of our church in a simple and seemingly minor manner. I call it The Mayonnaise Method.

Perhaps you know the slogan for Hellmann's mayonnaise—"Bring out the Hellmann's . . . and bring out the best!" While claiming to be the best mayonnaise, Hellmann's is also telling us that it brings out the best flavors in other foods.

This is certainly true for my taste buds. One reason I like Thanksgiving dinner so much is the leftovers. I make every attempt to wolf down my share of cold turkey sandwiches—if I can get to them before my kids do. The problem is that I like the white meat best, which does tend to be a bit dry. But a generous supply of mayonnaise enhances the flavor of the turkey, the crunch of the lettuce, and the texture of the toast. The mayonnaise itself is almost forgotten for the strength of the rest. But without the mayonnaise, it is an unhappy event. With it, there are few meals (or snacks) I like better.

When we use The Mayonnaise Method, we bring out the best in other people. We draw out their strengths without drawing attention to ourselves. Encouraging others to use their gifts for the good of the church is every bit as important as chairing committees or leading the singing or teaching a Sunday school class.

One of the simplest yet most effective ways to do this is to express appreciation for the character we see in people.

"Thank you for being so cheerful."

"I've always appreciated your stick-to-it-iveness."

"Your patience is amazing!"

Deciding to affirm one person like this each week at church can have a powerful effect. I can motivate dozens of people to continue living Christlike lives, when they may feel tired and discouraged underneath.

A dose of honest affirmation can transform a person. I've seen it happen many times. One day at lunch I made a point of telling Walt—a friend known for being, shall we say, a bit negative—that I appreciated all he had done and how well his work reflected on all of us. Walt was a different person all afternoon. He was positive, upbeat, and constructive about the job at hand.

Praise has mysterious powers. I have watched how the use and abuse of affirmation has tilted the outcome of more than one volleyball game. Those teams that cheer the efforts their members make and don't step in to take away shots from each other find themselves on top of more talented teams who carp, complain, and criticize each other at every flub, flaw, and fault.

A simple, well-placed comment of affirmation, perhaps combined with a suggestion, can also have profound effects.

"Bill, when are you going to join the choir? They can always use basses as good as you are."

"Sue, did you ever think of putting your business sense to work as treasurer for the church retreat?"

"You seem to have such a concern for homeless people, Henry. What could you do to help the rest of us understand what's going on?"

The point of the suggestion is not to manipulate people or make them feel guilty. It is to give folks an idea of how their gifts might be put to practical use for the benefit of all.

Some Christians think we shouldn't affirm people because it will go to their heads. But our job is not to keep people humble. That is the Lord's business. Rather, He has given us the task of building up each other in Him, confirming the spiritual gifts we see in action and thanking them for their good work.

Paul's letters are full of praise for what individuals did. The last chapter of Romans, for example, is devoted to praising people and their deeds—Priscilla and Aquila for risking their lives, Mary for working hard, Urbanus for being a fellow worker, Apelles for being tested and approved in Christ; and the list goes on.

People tend to live up to our expectations of them. When we speak positively about them, their own view of themselves is affected. They change and grow under our influence. With The Mayonnaise Method, we bring out the best.

Hardcore Worship

Jack Hayford

There's a central core of pivotal possibilities in everyone of us. This "center of being" so foundational to each of us is interchangeably called the "heart" or "spirit" of man. It's our heart because it's central to our life and effective function and because it determines our primary focus, interests, and affections. It's our spirit because it's central to touching God—the Source of our life and Resource of power to live it. Our worshiping the Almighty God is the key to activating and revitalizing this "core." Our worship "connects" us with Him:

- Like a landsat uplinks to capture a picture and message from a satellite in space.
- Like an elevator built into the hub of a high-rise allowing contact and interaction at every floor level.
- Like a ski lift takes us from the plain of the mundane to the peak of adventure.

I had just finished a workshop on worship. Jack Neely, a tough-but-gentle, strong-but-quiet guy—a contractor in the roofing business and committed disciple of Jesus Christ—had been there as I'd outlined the principles of power "When a Man Worships." Like so many of the hundreds of men I meet with monthly, Jack was getting a hold of the fact that spirituality isn't mystical; that operating in continual touch with the Immortal, Invisible Almighty God isn't a lapse into mindlessness or bizarre behavior.

We'd just looked at Abraham, who the Bible says "fathered" the way of faith for men like us, and among the power-principles

149

we noted in Abraham's worship was the power of his footsteps. God told him, "Walk through the land I've promised you!" Abraham had done it because he believed his obedience was an act of worship, moving in to possess God's promised boundaries for his life. Jack's mind was gripped by this revelation in God's Word, reminding him that the worship of his heart—now spiritually reborn through his receiving Christ—was more than a devotional exercise. He was learning that as a man worships his Creator, his spirit—his inner being—is endowed with a "weight of glory." He saw how that "weight"—a pure vein of Heaven-born substance to his life, filling the center of his being as he worships—is intended by God to be a dynamic for dealing with practical daily issues.

Jack and Julie had been having trouble with their teenaged daughter, Cathy. A good kid had suddenly begun behaving strangely. A rebellion not present before was starting to stress the family's relationship with Cathy, and strained moments were crowding into a happy home.

Armed with this lesson on the power in the faith-filled footsteps of a worshiping man, Jack rose early the next morning before the family or neighbors were up and about. In the dim light of that predawn hour, he went outside and began to walk the property line bounding their home site. As he stood at each corner, he lifted his hands in praise to the Almighty, then strode forward with worship, doing two things: First, he declared the might and glory of God, expounding on His greatness, power, and love. Second, he called on God's power to surround his home—overrule any evil power seeking to penetrate the boundaries of this family's life. Jack's worshipful action was rewarded with incredible speed and precision.

Later that morning, Jack had hardly left for work and Cathy for school when Julie, while standing at the sink washing the breakfast dishes, was impressed in her mind with a clear picture. She saw herself entering her daughter's room, opening a specific drawer, reaching to the back of the drawer under specific garments, and finding a small packet. She sensed God's presence prompting her and quickly dried her hands and did exactly what she had just seen. The result was the discovery of a package of marijuana, obviously hidden by their daughter.

When Cathy arrived home from school, Jack and Julie lovingly, but pointedly, confronted her. Jack first described how God had moved him to walk in worship around their home, inviting God's power—"Thy Kingdom come!" Next, Julie related her experience at the kitchen sink, and her pursuant action. Then, laying the small packet before Cathy, they expressed their love for her and their desire to help—words that were instantly met with a teenager's tears and overflowing words of repentance. "Mom, Dad, I didn't really want this stuff . . . I don't know why I've been like I've been . . . but I know this is Jesus' way of stopping me. Thank you . . . Thank you. . . ." And amid more tear-filled eyes, a family was bonded closer than ever.

It's just one example of the power of what I call "hardcore worship." It's the center of a man's being becoming filled with the solid gold of living praise. It's born of childlike humility in worship before the Creator. It's the "praise with understanding" that brings the dimension of divine blessing into practical daily application. And it discovers and invites the power of God's Kingdom, over and above the efforts of the darkness to crowd His glory-brightness from our homes or any part of our lives.

Keeping Your Roots Planted Deeply in Your Home Church

Luis Palau

When it comes to fast food, my wife, Pat, and I are of two completely different minds. She likes Burger King, I definitely prefer McDonalds. But that's okay. In such matters, variety is the spice of life.

Unfortunately, many Americans treat going to church much the same way they decide where to eat. "Let's see, we went to Dairy Queen last week, so let's go to Wendys this week." And off the family goes, blowing like an autumn leaf from one church to another.

As Christian husbands and fathers, I'm convinced it's crucial that we keep our family's roots planted deeply in our home church. Otherwise, if you and I remain shallow in this important area of commitment, we'll lose out on the support of other Christians when the storms of life hit.

By neglecting to minister within our home church, we also cause other Christians to lose something. The Lord Jesus says that He is the vine and we are connected to Him as branches (John 15:5-8). As a result, through Jesus, we are connected to each other. We are members of His Body, the Church.

In 1 Corinthians 12:26, we read, "If one part suffers, every part suffers with it; if one part is honored, every part rejoices with it." How you and I relate to the Body of Christ directly affects other Christians. We need each other!

My wife and I happen to be members of Cedar Mill Bible Church in Portland, Oregon. Although we travel quite a bit to speak at Christian conferences and evangelistic crusades around the world, we know we're not excused from taking an active part in the life and ministry of our home church.

Sure, we've heard about bigger and (possibly) better churches scattered here and there throughout the city. But, so what? The only valid reasons I can think of for leaving one's local church to go to another church would be heresy about a pivotal doctrine such as the divinity of Jesus Christ or the authority of the Bible; blatant immorality (theft, adultery, or whatever) rebelliously left undisciplined, unresolved, and ignored (1 Corinthians 5:11); spiritual deadness that threatens the spiritual vitality of one's children; or moving to another city, of course.

But since when is the church a country club where you pay your dues until you find something more exciting to do? Even though our home church (like all churches!) has its faults, we've gladly spoken well of it and especially made a point to do that in front of our sons. We found that helped them claim the church as their own when they got older.

One habit we have when getting ready to leave the house on Sunday morning is to take certain expectations about what we want to get out of church and leave them home with the dog. Our goal when we go to church isn't to get, but to give.

Whatever we do for the least of God's family, we actually do for Him. Don't wait until someone asks you to do something. Volunteer to serve in some capacity. Take the initiative to invite folks— especially singles—to join you for Sunday dinner. Show hospitality to your church's missionaries when they're home on furlough. As a family, visit the sick and the elderly. Take food to those facing financial difficulties.

Several years ago, a friend lost his job. Some months later, we heard that his family's house would be foreclosed if the payments weren't met. They had already sold their cars in order to meet their financial obligations. Pat suggested that we make one of their house payments. We invited others to help, too.

Together, as part of God's family, we can support each other in even the most difficult of times if our roots are planted deeply in the church.

Why Men Feel
So Out of Place at Church

Robert Hicks

A mother went into her son's room early one Sunday morning and tried to get him out of bed. After several attempts, she said, "Honey, you have to get up and go to church." He replied, "Give me one good reason why I have to go to church. The people at that church don't like me. Why should I go?" His mother declared, "Because you are the pastor!"

That's right. Even pastors feel out of place in church. I contend the reason is that the church—no matter what denomination—is essentially an institution that appeals more to women than to men. I am amused over all the current debate about ordaining women. It is as if women have never had any power in the church. But talk to any clergyman or look at most church records indicating percentages of men and women, and the truth comes out. Women exercise tremendous power in all churches by sheer numerical strength.

How can this gap be explained? During one Sunday morning service, I looked around and asked myself, Does anything here really attract men? Is anything here distinctively masculine? I noticed robes, flowers, and things being repeated that most men couldn't relate to.

By contrast, one of the most memorable communion services I have ever experienced was held in the Australian outback. Because there was no pastor, the men of the church took turns leading the communion service. A rugged miner was leading it the day I was there. He had all his notes on index cards, and in the middle of the ceremony, all the cards fell to the floor. He tried to regain his composure, made an unsuccessful attempt to put the cards back in order, and finally started crying. He sobbed, "I wanted to do such a good job for the Lord." I looked around; there wasn't a dry eye in the place. I said to myself, Isn't this what communion is all about, bringing our brokenness to the brokenness of Christ and finding the acceptance and forgiveness we so need in Him? After the service, we roasted an entire lamb on a spit and shared it.

The two images are far in distance and in concept. One service was flowery, formal, and predictable; the other was unpretentious and imperfect, with allowance for failure and human frailty. I would suggest one was feminine, the other masculine. What has brought about this large-scale feminization of the church, which makes men feel very much out of place? Some people might debate my observation on this point. Many men are "in church," but I am addressing whether or not they feel at home there.

I have seen too many good men leave the church, or church leadership, because they were tired of playing the games and they saw a lot of what the church was doing as a waste of time. We must recapture the church for men, defeminize it, and make our appeals to men where it will cost them something more than their money or their time. Christ wants their lives.

How do we reclaim men for the Kingdom of God and get them into the doors of the church? I wish I knew a surefire answer. But two images come to my mind. One is the sterile, cold, formal, flowery image of church with over half the audience women. The other image is the most recent Flyers hockey game I experienced, and I mean experienced! I looked at the audience, by far more men than women. What were they wearing? Anything! Some were dressed for the stock exchange; others for the Philly meat market. How did they behave? Were they passive, quiet, unemotional, refined gentlemen? Hardly. They were involved, vocal, upset, yelling, celebrating. I thought to myself, Here is a man's world, a place where he can let it all out, be himself, wear anything he desires, and they still let him in. And he actually pays to come! But what about the church? No, there a man can't be himself; he has to watch what he says, act appropriately, and wear a neatly pressed and coordinated suit and tie. Then it hit me: We're all dressed the way our mommies always wanted us to dress. We're all nice, clean little boys, sitting quietly so we won't get into trouble with our mothers!

Am I suggesting we turn the church into a hockey game? Of course not. (After all, someone might get hurt.) But I do know that men will come to something and pay for it when we identify with it. It's obvious we don't feel that way about church, so I continue to think about the hockey game.

9

The Promises You Make to Your Work

Gary Smalley and John Trent

U.S. diplomat W. Averell Harriman was known as a phenomenally hard worker who expected the same from his staff. There is a story that one afternoon he left his office at the unprecedented time of 5:30. "I'm not coming back tonight," he called to his staff, "so you can declare a half-holiday." All of us have known at least one employer like that; some of you may be employers like that. Unfortunately, we have also seen damage that can be created by our own workaholic attitudes and behaviors.

It's true that many men see the work they do as what defines their life. This book shows that what defines a man's life must be multifaceted. Men are most fulfilled in their work when it doesn't have to fulfill them. Of the marks of masculinity, self-confidence lends the most important help here. When we're assured of our worth in God's sight, we don't have to let our work define our inner self. This frees us to be our best, and not worry about what we do.

The work place is a key area of life. If we do a poor job, we will be handicapped in other important areas, like caring and providing for our families. Yet most of us have experienced hurt in the work place: broken promises, exploitation, being passed over. But focusing on those hurts is the wrong attitude to take. We must learn these lessons about the work place itself: (1) the way we work with others will show our true inner selves; and (2) being God's stewards means more than just working hard at a job—it entails our whole life. That means, for Christian men, we must seek to do our work as unto the Lord, and never shirk the other important responsibilities—our families—that God has given us watchcare over.

A Man and His Work

James Dobson

I n twentieth-century America, it is almost inevitable that a vig-
orous competition arises between a man's job and his home.
Achieving a balance between two areas of responsibility requires
constant vigilance, and quite frankly, most men tip the scales dramatically in the direction of their employment.

I have struggled to achieve a proper perspective between my
profession and my family. Just when I think I have conquered the
dragon of overcommittment, I say "yes" a few times when I should
have said "no, thanks," and the monster arises to maul me again. I
know of no easier mistake to make, nor one that has such devastating implications for the family.

The worst seige of overcommitment I've ever experienced came
once when I went through six weeks of incredible pressure, involving obligations that should have been spread over six months.

I had agreed to speak at various functions around the country
on five out of six consecutive weekends. At the same time, I was
facing deadlines on a new book, three new tape albums, a weekly
radio broadcast, and a random IRS audit (lucky me). Fatigue
mounted week by week, as I ran to catch planes, write speeches,
and search for tax receipts.

The climax occurred in early October, when I flew to Cincin-
nati to participate in a Praise Gathering, sponsored by Bill Gaither.
I lost a night of sleep going in, due to the time change, and then
spent two days standing before crowds ranging from two hundred
to eight thousand. It was an exhilarating time of teaching and sharing and counseling, but it squeezed the last drop of energy from my

frame. As I staggered toward the airport in a state of utter exhaustion, one thought pulsed through my head, "It's over!"

Let's leave that westbound plane for a moment and journey to a home in Arcadia, California, where my wife, Shirley, is also approaching the end of a siege. For six long weeks she has run the home without benefit of a man. It has been her task to discipline, train and guide, feed, medicate, and bathe two rambunctious kids. Needless to say, she is also near the point of exhaustion. Furthermore, Shirley has hardly seen her husband since the first of September, and her emotional needs have been on a prolonged "hold." One thought gives her strength to continue: "At last, Jim is coming home, and he'll take over!"

It takes no great analyst to observe that Shirley and I approached that final weekend on a collision course! Each of us was too exhausted to consider the needs of the other.

I arrived home on Friday night, and Shirley greeted me warmly at the door. We chatted about recent events and the kids and routine matters before sleep overtook us. The next morning went smoothly enough . . . at least until breakfast was over. As we were finishing the meal, our attitudinal differences suddenly blew up in our faces.

"Uh, Jim," said Shirley, "as you know, seventy-five members from the Singles Department at our church will be using our house tonight, and I need you to help me get ready for them. First, I want you to wash down the patio umbrella."

My blood pressure immediately shot up to about 212, and steam began to curl from my ears. Didn't Shirley know how hard I had worked? What kind of a slave driver was this woman? Didn't she understand how much I needed this day? Well, I'll tell you something! I'm watching that football game, and if Shirley doesn't like it she can just lump it!

So I had my way. I watched the football game in my study, but the tension around me was incredible. Silence prevailed between husband and wife. Not a word had been spoken since our terse interchange in the backyard. Then our anger began to turn into mutual hurt, which is even more damaging to communication.

The seventy-five church members came that evening and were served refreshments on the patio. They didn't seem to notice the dirty umbrella. They eventually departed, leaving me in the company of a mute female who still acted like the entire episode was my fault. Isn't that just like a woman?

Then came the awkward time of day called bedtime. I climbed into my side of the kingsize bed and parked as close to the edge as possible without plunging over the precipice. Shirley did likewise, clinging tenaciously to her "brink." At least eight feet of mattress separated us. No words were spoken. There were, however, frequent sighs from both parties, accompanied by much rolling and tossing. Shirley finally got up to take two aspirin and then returned to bed. Fifteen minutes later I turned on the light to put some drops in my nostrils. What followed was one of the worst nights of sleep in my life.

The next morning was Sunday, which presented more uncomfortable moments. We dressed and went to our adult class, still bearing deep wounds and resentment. And wouldn't you know, the teacher chose that morning to talk about marital harmony and God's plan for husbands and wives. Shirley and I nodded and smiled in agreement, but we felt like kicking each other under the table. It made me suspect that many other couples were also putting on a good front to hide their real feelings.

I wish I could say that the problem was resolved on Sunday afternoon, but such was not the case. Nor did it end on Monday or Tuesday. By Wednesday morning, we were sick to death of this silent warfare. We were both more rested by that time, and the issue began to lose some of its fire. I told Shirley I wanted her to join me for breakfast at a restaurant, and announced my intention of going to work late.

What occurred was a beautiful time of communication and love. I began to see that Shirley was in the same state of need that I had been. She began to understand the depths of my fatigue. We talked it out and reestablished the closeness that makes life worth living. Not only did we survive the crisis, but we learned several valuable lessons and grew from the experience.

Let me now share with you the biggest lesson that came from this experience: *Overcommitment is the number-one marriage killer.* Perhaps this will assist you in handling a similar episode in your marriage.

This lesson teaches us several things. Not only are fatigue and time pressure destructive to parent-child relationships, but they undermine even the healthiest of marriages. How can a man and woman communicate with each other when they're too worn out even to talk? How can they pray together when every moment is programmed to the limit?

From this vantage point, I have to admit that my fight with Shirley was primarily *my* fault. Not that I was wrong in wanting to rest after arriving home. But I was to blame for foolishly over-commiting my time during that period. The conflict would never have occurred if I had not scheduled myself wall to wall for six weeks. My lack of discipline in my work caused Shirley and me to become exhausted, which brought a chain reaction of negative emotions: irritability, self-pity, petulance, selfishness, and withdrawal. Few marriages can survive a long-term dose of that bitter medicine.

Many men already know that it isn't easy to implement a slower lifestyle. Prior commitments have to be met. Financial pressures must be confronted. Also, we must not overlook that ever-present masculine need to succeed, to push, to strive, to accomplish.

Besides, isn't everyone else doing the same thing? Sure they are. I don't even know any men who aren't running at a breathless pace—my physician, my lawyer, my accountant, my handyman, my mechanic, my pastor, my next-door neighbor. There is symbolic sweat on the brow of virtually every man in North America. Most of these husbands and fathers will admit that they're working too hard, but an interesting response occurs when this subject is raised. They have honestly convinced themselves, and will tell you with a straight face, that their overcommitment is a result of temporary circumstances. A slower day is coming. A light shines at the end of the dark tunnel.

Unfortunately, their optimism is usually unjustified. It is my observation that the hoped-for period of tranquility rarely arrives. Instead, these short-term pressures have a way of becoming sandwiched back to back, so that families emerge from one crisis and sail directly into another. Thus, we live our entire lives in the fast lane, hurtling down the road toward heart failure. And what is sacrificed in the process are the loving relationships with wives

161

and children and friends who give life meaning.

I, for one, have examined America's breathless lifestyle and find it to be unacceptable. Why should we work ourselves into an early grave, missing those precious moments with loved ones who crave our affection and attention? It is a question that every man and woman should consider.

Let me offer this final word of encouragement for those who are determined to slow the pace: once you get out from under constant pressure, you'll wonder why you drove yourself so hard for all those years. There is a better way!

Traveler's Advisory

Ken Abraham

R emember when travel used to be fun? Back before you began traveling for a living?

You're not alone. Modern men, in a variety of occupations, are finding the demands of business-related travel to be exhausting, exasperating, but inevitable.

Anybody who has ever been on a five-thirty flight or a rush-hour subway knows business travel is no fun. It's hectic, harried, and downright hazardous to your health: physically, emotionally, and spiritually.

Many a good, godly man has succumbed to the subtle snares of temptations encountered during job-related travel. Nowadays, we almost expect frequent travelers to be unfaithful to their wives. I was discussing this with a salesman sitting next to me during a flight to New York, when he said sardonically, "Marital infidelity goes with the territory. It's sort of an occupational hazard."

How sad that adultery has become an "acceptable risk" among business travelers. But sexual immorality, as prevalent as it may be, is only one of the devil's devious devices designed to destroy the frequent traveler. Many others are equally devastating: Self-indulgent vices such as over-eating, "throwing back a few brewskies with the boys," viewing dirty movies "in the privacy of your hotel room," or surrendering to loneliness, self-pity, or laziness. Things you would reject immediately at home somehow seem acceptable on the road.

Most Christian men know these indiscretions are not Christlike, yet at times, we all feel powerless to overcome them. Perhaps you too have wondered, "How can a Christian man beat the 'on the road again' blues?" Here are three tips that have helped me:

Keep Your Spiritual Priorities Straight

The Bible presents a specific pattern for appropriating power over temptation: "Submit therefore to God. Resist the devil and he will flee from you" (James 4:7, NASB). Notice the order: first submit to God, then resist the devil.

Most of us, in our misguided ideas of macho self-sufficiency, have reversed the order at times, only to suffer humiliating defeat. Then, after having been thoroughly embarrassed, we have blamed our spouses, the boss, the territory, or even God for our failures, frustrations, and foolishness.

The biblical principle is seek God's help first, not after all other efforts have proven futile and ineffective. To do so, it helps to have a Bible along with you on the road. Surprisingly, many men who wouldn't think of leaving home without a credit card travel without their first line of protection, the Bible.

Take your Bible with you and read a bit each morning. Then, at the end of a tough day, instead of turning on the tube, turn to the Word of God for some spiritual insight and inspiration. Remember, the devil doesn't go on break when you go out of town.

Avoid Temptation

This applies especially in areas where you know you are weak. A friend of mine, who is a professional athlete, says he is most vulnerable to temptation when the team first gets back to the hotel after a game.

"Following a game, I may be happy and loose if we won, or I may be angry and depressed if we lost. Either way, I am not immune to the lure of the attractive women who congregate in our hotel lounges, or the free-flowing liquor, or simply the relaxation of having a few laughs with my teammates who I know will be gathering for post-game libations.

"Right there, I must make a conscious choice to step inside the elevator, go up to my room, and call my wife."

Maintain Accountability

The athlete's precaution illustrates a third helpful tip for the frequent traveler. Whenever he travels, he knows that his wife is expecting his phone call soon after the game concludes.

My wife and I do something similiar. Most nights while I am on the road, I call home, usually shortly past eleven o'clock to take advantage of lower telephone rates. Besides building anticipation and dulling the edge on our loneliness, the phone calls create an accountability for both of us. Our conversations are not normally earthshaking. Frequently, we simply review the events of the day. Sometimes, we pray together over the phone. Often, our calls echo Stevie Wonder's song, "I Just Called to Say I Love You." But the calls keep us connected and accountable.

Frequent job-related travel can take its toll on the best of us, but by incorporating these few tips you can make work-related travel work for you.

No Compromise

Jay Carty

A dear friend, who had a one-man ministry after which I patterned Yes! Ministries, gave the best single piece of advice anyone has ever given me. "Jay," he said, "don't take the first $5." He was telling me not to compromise a little, because a little almost always leads to a lot.

I was put to the test early in the ministry and have continued to be tested monthly thereafter. When I speak at churches, tapes and books are usually sold. A certain amount of the proceeds are in the form of cash. Naturally the cash is untraceable.

What is there to keep me from pocketing the dollars? Absolutely nothing. No one would ever know. Not the IRS, not my board; no single person would ever know . . . except me—and God. And that's what my friend was warning me about. Because after the first time, it's just a matter of zeros—$5 becomes $50, $50 becomes $500, and so on.

One month I was a little short of money. That's when pocketing the cash is real tempting. I put $64 from tape sales in my wallet and used it to get home without entering it in the books. Over $40 remained burning in my britches five days later. Was I actually going to compromise the ministry for $64? I couldn't stand it, took out my check book, made up the difference, and put that money back into the ministry. And no, I didn't claim a deduction for my check written to Yes! Ministries, because it wasn't a gift. I was paying back a debt.

Once I purchased a "walkman" to listen to tapes on planes and in airports when I travel. It was a justifiable expense in my mind at the time, but it was a "no-no" for Jay. I tried to rationalize for two weeks before I wrote a check back to the ministry. I thank God for the loudness and persistence of His voice. He hasn't allowed me to keep the first $5.

There are many ways to take $5. I cheated on a test in college once. I had to get a 3.6 to keep my graduate scholarship and I caved in to the pressure. It's interesting, I got a C. The next quarter, in the second sequence of the class, I prepared properly, took the same professor's test and got an A on the final. The professor accused me of cheating because the paper was so different from the quarter before. I learned a valuable lesson—the hard way. That first dishonest act is the same as taking the first $5.

A senuous conversation, glance, or touch with someone other than your spouse is the first $5. Played out it leads to adultery. The first lie to stay out of trouble is the first $5. It's not long until lying becomes comfortable. The first pack of gum lifted from your local 7-11 is the first $5. Unchecked it leads to stealing items valued with more zeros—and jail.

We lived next to a Navy base for years. There's an interesting military term called "comshaw." It's what military surplus is called after someone has taken it. The practice was so common it was no longer considered stealing. It was comshaw.

That kind of thinking made the Iran/Contra arms scandal and Watergate okay at the time. It's comshaw when you do it, but it's stealing when you get caught; it's politics when you do it, but it's illegal when you're found out. In the light of day it's clearly wrong; but as a continued compromise it's just an extension of what you've grown used to doing as a way of life. The whole PTL situation was a result of the first $5 having been taken and not returned. After the first $5 it just became a matter of zeros—six of them, in fact.

Hey, Dad! Take a lesson here. Don't take the first $5. Don't compromise.

In Search of Integrity

John E. Brown III

I had an unusual call recently from a graduate of our college. He just wanted to let me know, he said, that some twenty years earlier he had cheated on one examination in a business course. He had gained a copy of a blank test to use in studying.

"It probably didn't make a difference in whether or not I passed the course," he said, "but it certainly helped my grade. It has been a growing burden on my conscience for the past few years. I am a Christian, and I just felt the need to tell someone there at the University about it."

I remembered reading a recent newspaper report about cheating at a large state university. Eighty-one percent of the students surveyed admitted to cheating one or more times during the year. A spokesperson for the university assured the press that the results were "not that much different from results of similar surveys taken at other universities."

I told this person on the phone that the University would seek no recourse against him (though it did occur to me to suggest a gift to the University's scholarship fund as the price for absolution). Then I asked what kind of work he was doing now. "Well, I'm the cash flow manager for (name) International Airport. I handle a portfolio of about $350 million."

Rolling my socks back up and breathing deeply, I said, "The Lord has certainly prepared you for that responsibility. The airport's money is in trustworthy hands."

A recent article in the *Wall Street Journal* on the "underground economy" reported these startling estimates:

1. Among self-employed workers, who do not have taxes withheld, only 41 percent of taxable income is reported to the Internal Revenue Service.

2. The Treasury estimates that in 1981, collected taxes should have been $90 billion higher than the amount actually paid. Primary methods of cheating include unreported income ($52 billion), overstated expenses and deductions ($13 billion), and illegal income from drugs, gambling and prostitution ($9 billion).

It is not just the feds that we cheat, however. We also cheat each other and our employers. Favorite devices include use of company equipment (telephone, copying machine, autos, etc.) for personal business, calling in "sick," and the old standby of padded expense accounts. More direct losses are attributable to theft of company supplies, tools or inventory.

Less apparent are the losses from wasted time on the job, unnecessary overtime, and other more "creative" ways of gaining something that is not earned. If the corporate climate routinely overlooks such behavior, it becomes an accepted, or even acceptable, employee practice. A few items of personal business at company expense is "the least they can do for me after all that I do for them. Besides, everybody does it now and then."

Cheating at anything is a slippery slope. Once the boundaries of honesty have been breached, moral judgments become obscure. A few dollars may become hundreds and thousands more.

An employer hiring or promoting a person to handle a cash portfolio of $350 million—or an expense account of $350—will try to find the man or woman who believes that the small things are just as important as the big ones. The evidence seems to indicate that such persons are not easily found.

But That's Not Good Business

Donald R. Harvey

When my daughter was in the seventh grade, her English teacher liked giving students challenging essay assignments. Paige had the opportunity of writing on such topics as: "What I like about myself," "What I would change in the world," and "What I think about my parents." She was also asked to write an essay on the color "green."

Creatively, Paige chose to associate "green" with food. What followed was a humorous assessment of green foods from the vantage point of a young adolescent. Green beans were stringy. Spinach was gritty. Broccoli smelled terrible. And lettuce could never be chewed up finely enough to be swallowed easily. Her evaluation wasn't flattering. As a color, green was okay. But as a food, it was lousy! Paige's theme was, When it comes to food, there's no place for the color green.

Some Christian businessmen could make a similar claim. For them, we would substitute integrity for the color green, and the context of the work place for food. They too have a theme. As a quality, integrity is okay. But it has no place in business.

Integrity connotes virtue, moral soundness, and honesty. All of these should be as much a part of a man's being as breath itself. Yet, far too often integrity seems disposable. Like the color green, there may be times when having integrity is okay, but at other times it's just not "good business."

One such occasion prompted a letter from the apostle Paul to Philemon, his "friend and fellow worker." Paul was writing about Onesimus, a runaway slave who had become a Christian under his ministry. Paul had convinced Onesimus to return to Philemon, his lawful owner. In his letter Paul's appeal was for Philemon to consider what difference their mutual faith in Christ would mean. Paul's words, I imagine, could have been something like this:

> Think about this from a different point of view, Philemon; not just from a cultural perspective, which legitimizes your right to view Onesimus as a piece of property, but from a Christian perspective, which demands a different outlook.

Paul may not have been actually asking Philemon to free Onesimus from slavery. But Paul clearly expected Philemon to accept Onesimus back without retribution (though he had every legal right to punish him) and the relationship between him and his slave to be significantly changed.

> For perhaps this is why you lost him for a time, that you might have him back for good, no longer as a slave, but as more than a slave—as a dear brother, very dear indeed to me and how much dearer to you, both as a man and as a Christian. (Philemon 15-16, NKJV)

I tried to imagine Philemon's response if he were living today. Unfortunately, what I came up with wasn't encouraging: "I hear what you are saying, Paul, but what you're asking for just isn't good business." Business in the nineties seems more concerned with what can be gotten away with than it is with what is right. And it seems more often to involve manipulation, half-truths, and misleading information than honesty.

I'm not suggesting that Christians practice bad business. But good business includes more than just the "bottom line." There's more to it than getting what you want "at all costs." There is integrity.

For the Christian, good business must expand beyond the merely legal to encompass the truly ethical. We can't segment our lives, living with integrity in one area and without it in another. (A Christian businessman is honest at home, at church, and in business.) Being a Christian does make a difference!

10

The Promises You Make
to Your Neighbors and Community

Gary Smalley and John Trent

T here is an ever-widening circle of responsibilities we have as we seek to be the kind of men God wants us to be. In this book we started with God, moved to ourselves, then to our wives. With these, our intimacy should be the greatest. Then comes family, those with whom we worship, and our friends.

Our next circle of interaction is with our fellow workers, our neighbors, community, and nation. Remember Jesus' words, "You will be my witnesses in Jerusalem, and in all Judea and Samaria, and to the ends of the earth" (Acts 1:8).

We have noticed, in many cases, that men fear leadership and taking responsibility in their communities. The problems at the national level of leadership in the U.S. are well documented: graft and corruption in politics, insider-trading on Wall Street, corporate espionage, and scandals in the religious community.

Most men perceive taking responsibility in the community and national arenas as involving enormous hassles and more personal sacrifice than they are capable of. Many also realize that power corrupts, families are lost, and egos crushed when we take the risks of broad involvement with others. Some shy away from community action or national leadership, then, for good reasons.

But God's word encourages us to be good citizens. We know that He puts the rulers in authority (Romans 13:1-7) and He asks us to submit to them because of our Christian conscience. As you read through the articles in this section, evaluate your own gifts and abilities, and ask God if He might use you in a more significant role in your community and your nation.

People First

Chuck Miller

Too often we forget that issues are people. We throw up our hands at our inability to affect the debate. Yet, by remembering that behind every issue, no matter how important or controversial, are real people—people whom Christ loves and longs to have a relationship with—we can have an impact.

In the 1960s, no issue was more controversial than school desegregation. Following a Sunday morning service, a woman stopped me and mentioned that she and her husband had attended the church for a few weeks and enjoyed the services. She said that her husband was not a Christian but respected me. I asked what her husband did, and she told me that he worked for the school district. She also mentioned that as a result of his responsibilities he was at the very center of the community's school integration issue. I told her that I would like to meet her husband. We arranged for the three of us to have lunch.

The lunch lasted almost two hours. I listened to the burdens of a man whose name was in the public debate daily. I asked about his relationship with Christ. He stated that he was a self-made man, who at thirty-five had never considered Jesus. I asked him if he was afraid that if he accepted Jesus Christ, he would become bored. Did he feel the Christian life was boring? He nodded yes. I then asked him to share with me the last two weeks of his life. I then shared with him the last two weeks of my life and told him that I found the Christian life anything but boring. He soon had to return to work, so he excused himself. I stayed and spent a little more time with his wife. She asked if I was aware of what had just happened. She said that her husband was never at a loss for words, but after he and I had finished comparing schedules, he was quiet. Too quiet.

A couple of weeks later, the man at the center of the most controversial issue of his day came to Christ. He and I spent time together. Although in the midst of heavy responsibilities and a heightened work load due to an impending federal court hearing, he made time to read the Bible. In fact, in his first four months as a Christian, he read from Genesis to Jeremiah. I was with him in the courtroom as the hearing began. At a break just prior to when he would be called to the witness stand to explain and defend his work, we walked down the hall and slipped into a corner to pray. Upon our return, he took the stand to begin his testimony.

What is community? It is people—people whom God invites us to come alongside. What do godly men do in community? They come alongside one another, and they pray. Who is someone in your community you might call today or reach out to and extend the friendship of Christ? What issues are you praying about? Who has God put into your life to pray for?

How has God made your life exciting in the past two weeks?

"God created . . ." (Genesis 1:1); "You are the light of the world" (Matthew 5:14).

Moral Collapse

Gary Oliver

I will never forget the day my little four-year-old son came home and asked my wife and me what a certain obscene four-letter word meant. I couldn't believe it! I don't remember hearing that word until I was in second grade. When I asked where he had heard it he replied that a little boy in his church preschool had said it, "and the teacher got real mad."

It was only fifty years ago that the movie *Gone with the Wind* was released and the nation was shocked when Clark Gable uttered the now-famous phrase, "Frankly, my dear, I don't give a damn." Times have changed. Standards have changed.

C. S. Lewis said, "Moral collapse follows upon spiritual collapse." There are many signs all around us that point to the fact that our nation is facing a moral crisis of major proportions. It is painfully clear that while some people are facing financial bankruptcy, our entire nation is facing a period of moral bankruptcy.

Webster defines *moral* as "of or relating to principles of right and wrong in behavior," and "conforming to a standard of right behavior." When I was growing up in the fifties and sixties most people still believed in absolutes. That simply means that there are some things that are always right and some things that are always wrong. While the United States was not a Christian nation, the morality of most people was based on the Judeo-Christian ethic. That was before Vietnam, Watergate, the deification of the first amendment, Jim Bakker, Michael Milken, and the savings and loan scandal.

Today few of us believe in absolutes. The present standard of morality is situation ethics. With situation ethics there are few things that are always right or always wrong. The only absolute is that a person should do the loving thing. But since there is no absolute standard of truth there can be as many definitions of the "loving thing" as there are people. From this perspective the basic moral question becomes not what is right or wrong, but rather what is expedient, or "How much can I get away with that won't do much harm to too many people?"

There are many indications of the moral decline in our nation. One recent report entitled "The Ethics of American Youth: A Report on the Values and Behaviors of the 18-30 Generation" argues that there are "undeniable signs that moral fiber of our country is weakening and that, as this generation takes its place in society in decision-making positions, the situation is likely to get worse."

The sixty-page study asserts, "An unprecedented proportion of today's young generation lacks commitment to core moral values such as honesty, respect for others, personal responsibility and civic duty." Michael Josephson, who is one of the researchers, sees high school students who cheated on exams becoming jet airline mechanics who falsify maintenance reports. He sees legions of young job applicants claiming degrees they don't have to get jobs they aren't qualified for.

Some of the figures cited in the report include:

•A 1989 Gallup poll found that 89 percent of those ages eighteen to twenty-nine thought their generation was more selfish than previous generations. More than 82 percent believed their generation was more materialistic.
•A long-term UCLA survey of college freshmen found that in 1970, 39 percent thought financial success was important or essential. In 1989 the figure jumped to 75 percent. In contrast, in 1970, 82 percent of college freshmen thought that "developing a meaningful philosophy of life" was important; by 1989 the number was exactly half that, only 41 percent.
•Cheating is rampant on both high school and college campuses. Various studies have shown that, overall, about 75 percent of high school students admit to cheating, while about 50 percent of college students do.

It would be easy to go on listing even more statistics to sub-stantiate the crisis. It is important that we stay aware of the breadth and depth of the problem. We need to be aware of what our spir-itual adversary is doing to affect our hearts and minds. But I believe Satan is delighted when we spend most of our time dwelling on the problem to the exclusion of seeking God's direction on effective solutions. A much more important issue is, What would God have me do as part of the solution?

It's tempting to bemoan what we can't change and ignore what we can change. It is much more comfortable to focus on the break-down of our society's corporate morality than to allow the Holy Spirit to make us aware of our own personal moral failures. It is less threatening to discuss the shocking lyrics of some contempo-rary music than the sin of gluttony. We have to be willing to allow God to show us our contribution to the problem. This will then lead us to our part in the solution.

While there are a variety of factors that have contributed to this decline in morality, Josephson is convinced that we have only ourselves to blame. "It isn't our view that these are moral mutants. These are not people who had some genetic disposition toward immoral conduct. . . . So my view is this generation is the price we are paying for our own moral deterioration."

While there is a lot that we can't change, there are clearly some things that we can change. If we dwell on the influences that are beyond our control, we will become frustrated and discouraged. As we focus on the influences that are within our control we can become hopeful.

What are some small steps we can take to be part of the solu-tion? If you have read this far you have already taken the first step. That step is to be aware of and acknowledge the problem. Someone once said, "A problem defined is a problem half-solved."

Step two is to talk about it. Help others to become more aware. Charles Colson tells that old story about the man who tried to save Sodom from destruction. The city's inhabitants ignored him, then asked mockingly, "Why bother everyone? You can't change them." "Maybe I can't change them," the man replied, "but if I still shout and scream it will at least prevent them from changing me!"

Step three involves sitting down with your Bible and taking an inventory of what you really believe. Ask yourself, "What are the basics of my faith? What is the core of what I believe about God, who He wants me to be, and what He would have me do?"

Then make a list of what you believe are the key moral issues of our society, and prioritize that list. Ask yourself, "Of all the things I believe, what are the most important?" Put the most important ones at the beginning. Then, looking at that list, ask yourself, "Which of these standards are clearly taught in God's Word, and which reflect more of a cultural or personal preference?" Be honest.

In step four get even more personal. Ask yourself, "What are the areas in which I am the weakest? In what areas am I most easily tempted to compromise? What aspects of my life reveal the greatest inconsistencies?" In my own life, one of the easiest ways I've found to identify my potential "blind spots" is to look at which attitudes and/or behaviors I am most likely to minimize or excuse. In Romans 14 Paul talks about how easy it is to pass judgment on the weaknesses of others. But in verse 12 he reminds us that "each one of us will give an account of himself to God."

Step five is to do it! Let's make sure that with God's help we practice what we preach. Vance Havner said, "When it comes to a deeper experience of Christ, too many only deplore the lack of it; some discuss theories about it, a few describe how to have it, but too few demonstrate it." God wants us to demonstrate truth.

I wouldn't blame you for saying, "Dr. Oliver, that's too simple. How can God use little changes in me to impact my family?" Don't be fooled into thinking that little equals insignificant. And while the impact may not be immediate it will be long-lasting. Follow God's advice in Luke 16:10 and be faithful in the little things. I promise you that the long-term reality of your authenticity will expose the emptiness of the world's pseudo-morality.

Are we facing a moral crisis? Yes! Is it a major problem? There's no question about it! Can I as one person solve it? Of course not! Can God use me to make a meaningful contribution to the solution? Most definitely *yes*! Remember the words to the children's song taken from Matthew 5:16:

This little light of mine, I'm gonna let it shine,
Let it shine, let it shine, let it shine.

Beyond the Cheers

Chuck Miller

I was scared to make the call. It meant getting involved. Brad's mother had asked me to talk to her son, who had just been kicked off the soccer team on which one of my sons also played. Brad was not doing well in school, and he did not have a good relationship with his father. Soccer was the one bright spot in his life.

I picked Brad up, and we went to lunch. I asked him about soccer, and he blurted out that he was not on the team anymore because he had been kicked off. He was very angry at the coach. He felt misunderstood, that the whole world was against him. I told him that I wanted to be his friend, that I had watched him during the season and sensed that he was special. I asked him where he saw himself in terms of his overall standing in his class. Was he in the top 10 or 50 percent? The lower 50 percent? I was saddened when he said that he thought he was in the lower 50 percent. When I asked him why he felt that way, our conversation extended and deepened. I realized then how important the team was to him.

We discussed his going to the coach and admitting that he had let him and the team down as a result of his actions. I asked him if he could ask the coach to forgive him for what he had done. After a period of silence, he said that he did not think he could.

This was my moment. God's challenge to me to get involved. Here was the reason for the lunch, for his playing soccer, for his actions. To risk sharing my faith—to another man's son. I told him that I also did not think he could ask for forgiveness. I said that it seemed he had tried by himself to give direction and meaning to his life, but had failed. I talked about how he had hurt the God who had given him a strong body and a handsome presence by ignoring God and being ungrateful for his talents. I explained that the beauty of the news of Jesus Christ is that He moves our lives from a "try harder" playing field, to an "I live life through the power of God" playing field.

I could not believe what I saw when, in the car after lunch, he asked Christ to come into his life. I was absolutely staggered as I watched the Holy Spirit transform a tense, rebellious high school spirit into a soft and pliable spirit. I told him that I was excited about his decision, and I explained to him how to grow in Christ. As we parted, I asked if he was willing to tell the coach that he was wrong for what he did. He said that he was ready to ask for forgiveness, even if the coach did not put him back on the team or let him play in any more games.

Brad was allowed back on the team. When I arrived at the next game and saw him play, I stopped and gave God thanks. Through my son and our family sitting in bleachers and cheering our lungs out, God gave me the treat of touching a life for Jesus Christ. Is God calling you out of the bleachers?

> For Christ's love compels us. . . . He has committed to use the message of reconciliation. We are therefore Christ's ambassadors. (2 Corinthians 5:14,19-20)

11

The Promises You Make to Those in Need

Gary Smalley and John Trent

While in Colorado Springs for a taping of James Dobson's Focus on the Family radio program, we were privileged to meet a dynamic pastor from Virginia, Wellington Boone. Wellington was participating with us on a panel of twelve men who came together with Dr. Dobson and Coach Bill McCartney expecting to discuss masculinity, the current men's movement, and what it means to be a promise keeper.

What we didn't expect was the testimony of an African-American pastor to touch all of us so deeply. After being conceived out of wedlock, Wellington was shipped off to his grandparents until he was eight. And so he learned to survive on the streets of that New Jersey ghetto.

But despite the awful conditions of his childhood, Wellington lived in a home that honored God. As a young man he came to a knowledge of Jesus Christ that was to transform his life—when he learned the distinction between mental assent to Christianity and a deep, personal commitment.

God has given Wellington a zeal for transforming lives through bringing people to Christ and then teaching them how to live biblically. We were greatly touched by Wellington's knowledge of Scripture.

One of the dominant themes of Wellington Boone's message is reconciliation. And we thought it fitting that Wellington begin this chapter with his cry for revival in the inner city and his special call to both black and white Christians.

Revival in the Inner City

Wellington Boone

I n the inner city of Richmond, Virginia, as in cities across the country, a count is done periodically to determine how many murders are committed. Each time, it seems, there is a relentless climb in those deadly statistics, and each time most of those murdered are black.

The escalating number of inner-city black homicides is a tragedy, but there's more to it. Those who commit the murders are also black. Statistics are skyrocketing of black-on-black homicide, blacks who sell drugs to blacks, blacks who give AIDS to blacks, and black women who abort their babies. One thing is increasingly evident: the black community is dying by its own hand.

The word *genocide*, coined during the death purges of Adolph Hitler, indicates that Hitler's death-targets were determined by ethnic group. If he had had his way, he would have eliminated the Jewish people from the earth.

In the inner cities, death targets are also determined by ethnicity. According to many of the most oft-quoted black leaders, the agent of this genocide, directly or indirectly, is white America.

THE TRAGEDY OF BLACK SELF-GENOCIDE

I believe it is time we took a closer look at the whole issue of genocide in the black community, this time from a biblical perspective. Historically, white America has been far from innocent of wrongdoing concerning blacks, but if we insist on blaming whites for our bondage, we will have to look to them for our deliverance.

It is time to make it plain: It is the people of our race itself who are doing the killing. We don't have to be destroyed by whites. We are doing it ourselves. For the first time in history, a people is engaged in a relentless course of self-genocide.

Why do blacks murder one another? Why do they kill one another with drugs? Why do black mothers destroy their unborn children?

VISION FOR A CHOSEN PEOPLE

Early in our history, blacks fought bitterly against the killing of their people. Slaves escaped through the Underground Railroad so that they and their offspring would be free.

Today, many inner-city blacks have lost the kind of God-centered, generational vision that says life is something worth saving. Fathers are unable to give vision to their children. Black leaders have not given vision to their people.

As a result, the inner city has become dominated by man-centered substitutes like humanism, Islam, and black pride and nationalism. Blacks as an ethnic group do not know where they are going. All they can do is look for answers in the past, especially in blaming the way they were treated by whites. Disengaging themselves from the real problem—their abandonment of Jesus Christ—they look on helplessly as their families and communities disintegrate.

The Bible says that without vision, the people perish (Proverbs 29:18). The word *vision* means sight and seeing and indicates direction and goals. The word *perish* means a loss of motivation for living. Those without a godly vision embrace short-sighted, ungodly practices like prostitution, drug-dealing, stealing, and playing the numbers or the lottery. Even those who attend college or enter the business world wonder, "Who am I? What am I here for?"

Vision among a people group is not an option. God's creation of man was a fulfillment of vision. He created man for purpose. In God Himself are visions and dreams and reasons for existence, and He imparts this ability to His children.

When black men abandon their natural and spiritual responsibility to their children, they lose that impartation from God. The result is spiritual death—in them and in their children. They never find out from God why they are alive, so they are unable to pass down a godly heritage to their children.

Blacks will continue to be visionless, wandering in despair, until they find out who they are in the sight of God, until they realize that they can have a viable personal relationship with Him through His Son, Jesus Christ. They need more than government programs or even religion. They need a relationship with God, a consistent prayer life, and proper teaching that the Bible applies to every aspect of their lives.

No people can survive a plight of such magnitude unless they get themselves right with God. They must ask Him to change their thinking and purify their hearts. They must see themselves as equals at Jesus' feet and begin to intercede for a lost and dying world.

In every human being is a God-shaped vacuum, and only God can fill it. Each person must find his God-ordained destiny as an individual through knowing His Creator.

ETHNICALLY CONSCIOUS, NOT ETHNICALLY CONTROLLED

Instead of seeking God, some blacks try to find self-worth in their blackness, but no member of any race can take credit for his color. No one can take pride in his gender or the place where he was born. Those matters were decided by God in eternity. As Jesus said, "You cannot make one hair white or black" (Matthew 5:36).

It is not emphasizing blackness that sets men free. It is the anointing that breaks the yoke (Isaiah 10:27), and the anointing is neither white nor black. People need God. It is as simple as that.

I discovered years ago that I was insecure not because I am black or because people mistreated me or called me names, but because I didn't know the Lord. In Him is security. Once I took my responsibility for getting before God and getting to know Him, letting Him impart to me His vision for my life, then I received a sense of worth, because I had found the Lord, the Creator of worth. In Him is all sufficiency.

When a person of one race treats with contempt a person of another race, he is revealing weaknesses in his own character. When we know Jesus Christ, we can have compassion on someone who insults us, not try to justify ourselves by retaliation.

In the past, some blacks kept quiet when they were treated as inferiors just because they wanted to avoid a confrontation. We keep quiet because we know who we are in Christ. We know that nothing that another person can say about us changes the truth. We know that we have value because we know the one who created us.

It has not been popular among blacks to learn strength through humility. They have tried to learn strength through pride—in blackness, in achievement, in anything that seems to take away the pain. In their ignorance, they have thought the path to greatness was paved with hate, when in reality it is paved with love.

When someone is despised and reacts with hate, he is revealing that his own character is just as defective as the person who is attacking him. Someone who knows Jesus Christ knows that He was a person who was despised and rejected, yet He never hated in return.

Jesus made a choice to lower Himself from His position of unity with God the Father in order to reach out to mankind. When a black person volitionally chooses humility, he is entering a high calling, not a low one. He is rejecting his base instincts that tell him to hate. He is choosing to make himself of no reputation (Philippians 2:7), as Jesus did, so that God may exalt him. A Christian lives not to seek favor from man, trying to become acceptable to other human beings on their terms. Instead, his desire is to please God, and to love his fellow man.

Because I am sufficient in the Lord, I have His grace for any situation. I do not have to seek commendation or even respect from those who hate me, because I know who I am in Christ. I know there is a call upon my life. Others can think what they want about me. They can call me any name they can think of. They can mistreat me, and I will forgive them. I am not living unto them. I am living unto God.

Paul told King Agrippa, "I was not disobedient unto the heavenly vision" (Acts 26:19). When you are into ethnicity, that is an earthly vision. It brings no eternal satisfaction. We may be ethnically conscious, but we must not be ethnically controlled.

WARNING TO THE CHURCH

An alarm is sounding throughout the body of Christ. It warns of impending judgment on those who do not subscribe to the Word of God as the gauge for measuring all programs and philosophies. The church will never have its own cutting-edge solutions for the crises in the inner city as long as it bypasses God.

In the ancient world, each city was surrounded by walls, and access to the city was only possible by passing through certain gates. In time, these gates became not only a place for allowing travel but also a place for conducting all important business transactions and public discourse. They were the place where the city fathers gathered to make decisions that affected the entire population. Thus, whoever controlled the gates controlled the people.

The gates of America's inner cities have been captured by the enemies of the black community. Although these blacks and non-blacks would never admit it, those who control these gates believe in their hearts that blacks are inferior to whites. They have contempt for the black men who act like nothing more than studs, and they have found it easy to wrest control from them.

The only hope for black America is for people who know God—both blacks and whites—to recapture the gates of the city and restore a firm foundation for city life, one built on the rock of Christ. I am speaking of a massive spiritual revival that will sweep through the streets and wake up every sleeping saint. I mean a trumpet call that sounds the alarm and calls Christians to battle.

The church should be an army, presenting to the world God's standard of equality. Instead, much of the evangelical church has carried a banner of indifference, especially in the area of racial equality.

The white church finds it easier to accept blacks as singers than as ministers of the Word, to whose oversight they must submit.

The black church, in turn, has not presented enough biblical reasons for dealing with racism. It has not promoted reconciliation. At its worst, it has been a participant in black genocide. I know that is a strong statement, but before I close I will explain what I mean.

When blacks were delivered from slavery by a sovereign act of God, they discovered what it was like to be a chosen people. Taken captive by African Muslims and transported like cattle by white slave traders, they found themselves in a strange land. Once there, however, the slaves discovered a treasure. It was something in which to bask, and an inheritance to pass down to their children. It was something so rich that it carried their people through more than 300 years of bondage.

What these slaves discovered in America was a living God who loved them. He was a God whom they could please instead of one like their African gods who hated them and looked for excuses to destroy them.

The tradition of that faith carried them through emancipation, reconstruction, and the birth pangs of civil rights. Today, however, the pillars of faith that have upheld black Americans are beginning to crumble. As a result, many young, inner-city blacks are in rebellion against authority, including their parents, their pastors, if they attend church, and certainly the Word of God. Many have turned away from Christ to serve the idols of pleasure, promiscuity, and materialism. They have no conception of Jesus' teaching that it is a blessing to be reviled for His sake. They would rather kill than bless their enemies, and they are spiritually dying as a result.

CALL TO PRAYER

The plight of the inner cities demonstrates how desperately America needs another great awakening.

Prayer has been the catalyst for every major revival in history. The failures of the political, social, entertainment, homosexual, and occult movements confirm that the one movement that has been neglected is the only one that will succeed. It is time to bring exponential healing to the inner cities through prayer.

America needs a groundswell of grass-roots involvement in prayer. The church must understand the urgency of this call from the heart of God.

As a black pastor and campus ministry leader, I see black self-genocide as one of the most serious problems facing black and white America today. It is more threatening than a Mid-East war. It is more destructive than AIDS. It is the deadly internal hemorrhaging of the American people, and unless it is healed, we will no longer be able to survive.

Black self-genocide can be blamed on one institution of society more than any other. It is the fault of the church. When society is in trouble, judgment begins at the house of God, because only when the church is purified can it affect society. Repentance must come first to the church, before the church can speak with authority to the world.

SINS OF BLACK AND WHITE CHRISTIANS

The sin of the church, both black and white, is its rejection of the absolute sovereignty of God and His plan for saving society through His Son, Jesus Christ. He knows how to redeem the people of the inner city, but He is waiting for blacks and whites alike to return to Him and to His biblical standard.

The white church looked at inner-city problems and moved to the suburbs. The black church looked at inner-city problems and bought locks and chains. Many blacks in recent years have looked for assistance mainly from the civil government and from white people, and only occasionally from God. Who was left to help the poor, the lame, and the blind? People who deny the relevance of Jesus' bibliocentric answers: the Black Muslims, Planned Parenthood, the American Civil Liberties Union, and others. Their reaction against the biblical position has come in no small measure because they see the failings of those who say they are God's people.

The plight of the inner cities is one of the greatest opportunities God has ever had to manifest His power. Poverty, drugs, out-of-control sex, crime, venereal disease, abortion, murder. The problems cry out for a solution, but for the most part only the humanists have tried to solve them. Unbelievers have put the church to shame, because they have had a zeal to find answers to the problems of the inner cities, while the church has had a zeal mainly for itself.

Spiritual revival will require a return of brokenness to the church, an admission that only God can save this people. It will require a return of power—over fear, over sin, and over reluctance to preach to the people with signs following. It will require an understanding of the ways of God. As Paul said, "Where sin increased, grace increased all the more" (Romans 5:20).

Revival will require a commitment to the Bible and the biblical standard for life. People of the inner city lack vision because they lack knowledge. They lack knowledge because they are ignorant of truth, or know the truth and have rejected it.

Blacks are ignorant because their pastors have not preached to them the uncompromising Word. When churches emphasize the Spirit to the exclusion of the Word, or the Word to the exclusion of the Spirit, the change that comes in a new convert's life is not wholistic.

Residents of the inner city need all of God. We should be able to offer them words and deeds, teaching and miracles. Paul said, "For I will not venture to speak of anything except what Christ has wrought through me to win obedience from the Gentiles, by word and deed, by the power of signs and wonders, by the power of the Holy Spirit, so that from Jerusalem and as far round as Illyricum I have fully preached the gospel of Christ" (Romans 15:18-19, RSV).

The Holy Spirit does not come around to play around. He comes around to get down. He does not come around just so people who are already saved can get ther needs met. He also comes to save the lost and to restore the desolations of former generations (Isaiah 61:4). He comes to manifest Himself in the inner city with a power greater than anything we have seen. When the church gets right with God, the lost will see His power and run to Him to be saved.

Camouflaged Christians

Steve Diggs

On a recent trip to New York to see my publisher I met a cabby I'll never forget. He was an amiable, nice guy who really liked to talk.

At first everything was fine. But soon I noticed that his attitude had changed. As we drove, he began to tell me about someone who had cheated him out of some money. The more he talked the angrier he got. Then things got really weird. He started talking about hiring someone to beat this guy up. (I'm still not sure whether he was talking generically or offering me a paying job.)

After going on for a while, he looked in the rear view mirror and asked me what I thought he should do. I gulped hard and said, "It's really not a matter of what I think you should do. The real question is, What do you think Jesus wants you to do?"

Things got quiet for a moment. Then he said, "Are you a Christian; have you been born again?"

Surprised by his familiarity with the subject (and grateful that he hadn't hit me), I said, "Yes I am."

With that he turned around, swung his hand over the seat and said, "Praise the Lord! I'm a Christian too. Shake my hand!"

Had he known what I was thinking, he probably *would have* hit me. I was at once disappointed, hurt, and repulsed. If this man was in fact a brother, I felt he had let me down. He seemed chameleon-like, changing to adapt to whatever his current environment was. Had I responded to his question by saying, "Sure, you ought to have the pulp beaten out of that guy, and I'll be glad to do it for you," he might have hired me.

Jesus wants His people to be "instant in season and out of season." He wants us to be "salt" in a world that is muddled and unseasoned. He wants us to be mature men who lead and do not have to be led. He wants us to stand powerfully for the right. As Christian men who have families, churches, and businesses to lead, we cannot afford the luxury of having to be wet-nursed ourselves. Simply put, Jesus wants us to either get on or get off:

"I know your deeds, that you are neither cold nor hot; I would that you were cold or hot. So because you are lukewarm, and neither hot nor cold, I will spit you out of My mouth." (Revelation 3:15,16, NASB)

Don't our actions sometimes deny that we know God? What about the way we talk on the golf course with our unsaved friends? The opportunities we miss to be a witness? Or, the tactics we use to close a sale? Jesus points out that we risk facing a dangerous future if we insist on being inconspicuous (or cowardly) in our faith:

"Everyone . . . who shall confess Me before men, I will also confess him before My Father who is in heaven. But whoever shall deny Me before men, I will also deny him before My Father who is in heaven." (Matthew 10:32-33, NASB)

In the professional world none of us would tolerate a manager who refused to manage. We'd lose all respect for a coach who didn't set a disciplined example before his team. God expects no less from us. Listen to what the Hebrew writer had to say to a bunch of Christians who, like Peter Pan, refused to grow up:

For though by this time you ought to be teachers, you have need again for someone to teach you the elementary principles of the oracles of God, and you have come to need milk and not solid food. (Hebrews 5:12, NASB)

So what is our challenge as men? It is to grow up and act our spiritual ages. In a phrase, our goal should be to leave the woodpile higher when we depart this world than it was when we arrived.

Concern for Those Who Still Need Christ

Luis Palau

Six weeks before he died, Elvis Presley was asked by a reporter, "Elvis, when you started playing music, you said that you wanted three things in life: You wanted to be rich, you wanted to be famous, and you wanted to be happy. Are you happy, Elvis?"

Elvis replied, "No. I'm lonely as hell."

Rich. Famous. But lonely. At first Elvis' remark may seem offensive. But actually it's well put. Hell is a lonely place. For some very lonely people, hell begins here on earth.

Some Christians don't say a word to others about Jesus Christ and what He's done for them because they think the lost are happy "just the way they are." They apparently have no concept of what pain, suffering, hurt, guilt, and loneliness many of their work associates, neighbors, and acquaintances are experiencing.

Even when you and I are aware that someone is going through tough times, it's still easy to do nothing. I've been guilty of this. My next door neighbor several years ago was a young television personality. We would chat from time to time. But I didn't talk with him about the gospel. After all, I thought, he seems completely immune to the problems of life.

My neighbor's situation, however, abruptly changed. Joy was no longer evident in his face. He and his wife started driving separate cars to work. I could tell that their marriage was souring and felt the need to talk with him, but hesitated because I didn't want to meddle in his life. I went about my business and left for an evangelistic crusade overseas. After all, that was the polite thing to do.

When I returned home, I learned that my neighbor had killed himself. I was heartbroken. I knew I should have gone to him, asked how things were going, and tried to persuade him to repent and follow Christ. But because of false courtesy—because I followed a social norm—I didn't do it.

It's easy to make excuses for not persuading others to follow Christ. We say we don't want to be overbearing or offensive; we think we can't witness to someone because he or she will become angry. But if we approach life's situations fully convinced that we are to persuade others about Christ, we will have the courage we need. And we will discover that many people are surprisingly open to the gospel message.

I have found that some of the people I considered the most closed to the gospel often were the most receptive. Although outwardly they may have feared it, in their hearts they welcomed the message of the good news of Jesus Christ.

As Christian men, our responsibility is simply to be obedient and available for God's use. When our aim is to please God, we have the needed determination to persuade others, winsomely and gently, to follow Christ. That conviction gives direction and joy to life.

No matter where we work or what we do, we have an objective that stands above all else: with heartfelt compassion, to persuade others to follow Christ.

Let Men Be Servants

Udo Middelman

Few of us have ever met a true house servant. In the past, we are told, there were many performing all sorts of tasks at the master's command. Now we read about them in P.G. Wodehouse or see them on BBC programs. We have loosened that bond and live as free people with rights. The time of butlers is finished. Only waiters still serve, mechanics service our machines, and we create service jobs in the service sector.

We see the life of the servant as a thing of the past that required almost blind obedience, being at the beck and call of others, having no life of his own.

It is hard to understand that the Bible calls all of us to be servants. Maybe that is something for nurses, but not for doctors. Secretaries may be expected to work tirelessly. When we think about it, we could include cab drivers, a few full-service gas station attendants, and "lower" jobs that require little mental activity, but full dedication.

Jesus Christ came as a servant. He gave His life for us. He did not have a "normal" life, because He loved us and took on the form of a servant.

But He was not mindless, without a concern of his own, without a strategy, a purpose, or a goal. He was not unskilled, or pushed around by the demands of others. He did not just do what others asked Him to do.

His service expressed His will and ability to accomplish what was necessary. He knew exactly what was needed. He knew the problems and the solution. He managed to accomplish his task.

He taught us what is true and put our foolishness to shame. He served us well, for without His work there would be no true human life, no hope, no peace, and no new life in righteousness.

We easily feel guilty when we are told to be servants. We are all too often accused of managing our affairs, of interfering in the lives of others, of lacking in humility, of imposing our skill on nature to survive, to heal, to redirect the affairs of nature and men. Now we are told to scale back, to take second place, to let others tell us. We are called to become stewards of nature, of global populations, to let all people, skilled and not so skilled, have an equal voice.

Real servants are people with knowledge and skill. They serve by doing what few others can accomplish. Only Christ could die on the cross for our sins; only He could atone; only He could be the way, the truth, and the life.

Servants are not ashamed, but proud of their ability. They see the need to teach, to tell, to show what is true, efficient, just, and good. They step in because they have seen the right way and want to limit the painful results of the merely personal ways of others. In a fallen world of insufficiency, of pain, of death itself, servants cut right to the core of the problem with workable solutions. Good intentions alone do not heal a patient. Skill, devotion, and commitment are equally required. We serve through superior ability in all areas, not through false self-denial, guilt, and humility that deny God's calling to be man made in His image and engaged in His battles . . . to win, like Jesus, not to submit.

Wrestling with Unemployment

Luis Palau

D
o you know anyone who is out of work? Someone in your family? A friend? Perhaps you have wrestled with unemployment recently.

I found myself suddenly unemployed while trying to support my widowed mother and five younger sisters. In those days massive strikes shook my home country, Argentina. I was without work, without relief, without anything! So I can thoroughly understand the pain and hollowness a person feels when he's fired, laid off or on strike.

Unemployment creates unique family, financial, and even medical problems. It also prematurely exposes a person to the perils usually associated with middle age: weariness, carelessness, and confusion. These very terms describe many of the unemployed today.

What should a committed Christian do if he finds himself out of work? Rather than blame government—much less God—be proactive! I believe the Bible gives us several specific principles that relate to God's will when you're unemployed.

First, accept your unemployment, even though it may be difficult, and trust God to work it for good. The Bible tells us, "We know that in all things God works for the good of those who love him, who have been called according to his purpose" (Romans 8:28). About that verse Vance Havner comments, "Paul did not say, 'We understand how all things work together for good'; he said, 'We know that they do.'" That promise is a solid anchor when the storms of unemployment beat heavily against us.

Second, carefully plan how to use your extra time in the best way possible. In Ephesians 5:15-16 we read, "Be very careful, then, how you live—not as unwise but as wise, making the most of every opportunity."

If you are unemployed, I suggest you spend the first two hours of every day in Bible study and prayer. Spend the next three or four hours seriously looking for a job.

Third, minister to other people during your spare time. Organize a Bible study with others who are unemployed, and pray together. Spend time discipling new believers.

As an individual or group, use your afternoons to work for your church, help those in need, visit the elderly, or actively evangelize in your community.

God's Word says, "Let us not become weary in doing good, for at the proper time we will reap a harvest if we do not give up" (Galatians 6:9). I believe that God will compensate those who volunteer to help others if they do it for His glory.

Fourth, be a good steward of your time, energy, and possessions. Work together as a family to see how you can creatively use what you already possess to meet some of your needs— and even to help others.

Perhaps you have some land. Plant a garden! Perhaps you have certain talents that could be used to earn money. Use them!

In Matthew 6:33 we read, "Seek first his kingdom and his righteousness, and all these things [food, clothing, etc.] will be given to you as well." As we honor God in every part of life, we can be sure that He will supply everything we need.

If unemployment strikes, I challenge you to seek God's Kingdom and righteousness. Act on the principles outlined above and trust God to provide for your every need.

Where Others Fear to Tread

Udo Middelman

Men put their mark in history. We sign documents, paintings, and bills. Some of us remember when we first saw our name in print. We write books and show our identity with business cards. We introduce ourselves by name. We make statues of famous people. We quote important and knowledgeable people.

We don't see human life as the carpet of history. Events, both good and bad, are not inevitable. Situations and relationships can be affected. With the birth of each person, a new life and that of a family takes a different direction.

When a man dove into the icy waters of the Potomac a number of years ago to rescue passengers of a crashed plane, he lost his life; but he made the news, became a hero, stood out as a person, and rescued several helpless passengers.

We are part of a culture of interventionists. Our understanding of nature, history, and the human condition are shaped by the Bible. Our God is not found in earth or nature. He did not create both life and death. His character makes a difference between good and bad. He speaks through His Word, not through our feelings or democratic averages. He is moral. Political schemes of seeking approval are not His ways.

Religion usually binds people to the way things always are. They submit to the greater circle of life, nature, mud, and normality. The God of the Bible, by contrast, awakens courage. He calls us out of these finite, impersonal and mostly impassionate things.

For the Bible tells us that we live in a world of need. We live after the Fall. Normality, as it is now, is not what God had in mind. Thorns and thistles are to be repelled, floods harnessed, death fought, and justice sought. Biology alone is not to govern our human relationships. The norms of God are not the same as statistically normal behavior of people or things.

We are not satisfied with an explanation. We also search for a solution. That search makes people cross oceans, defy bacteria in surgery, look for resources under the ground and for change in every hostile and inhuman situation. It responds to the basic curiosity of the child, the quest for knowledge and rightful dominion. It is the outworking of our identity as persons. But it is only justified in light of the Bible.

God thinks it is important to put food on the table. Shelter is urgent in an inhospitable world. The world needs to be measured accurately, so that ships can go and return with cargo. Planes fly only when we dare to be precise, when getting there is important. Paintings should give a true perspective. Marriages are worth a lifetime of investment, struggle, admission, and forgiveness for the sake of a unique relationship.

Against the opposition of nature, we harness water, wind, and fire. Even the light of the sun gets squeezed through a wire into the lights of our homes, factories, and hospitals. We dare to demand a longer day to work, to read, and to produce than would naturally be ours in winter months.

We dare to tread without fear because we are God's children, not nature's pawns. We are stewards of our high calling as people made in God's image. We do not sacrifice individuals, neighbors, and children to an idea of a better harmony of nature and the human race.

You matter—to God. He intervened with power, moving the earth and using the womb of Mary. He stilled the water when it threatened to sink the disciples. He called up a huge storm and the waters were parted to make room for Israel's men, women, and children, avoiding Egypt's anger.

You matter—to yourself, your family, your world. Without your choices a broken, fallen history would continue without compassion, without skill, without morality, consuming human lives in the normal cycles of nature. Your dignity demands expression. What religions and nature do not tolerate, the Bible demands. They make prisoners of human beings. They crush the spirit of enterprise and responsibility. They steal the hope. They breed indifference, an embrace of fate.

But God calls you to be a man, to go where other men fear to tread.

12

The Promises You Make to the Future

Gary Smalley and John Trent

It took only a split second that cool, August night in Candlestick Park. Ninety feet due north of home plate, Dave Dravecky's future snapped in the instant it took for his arm to break. All of his comeback dreams, all his carefully laid plans. With a "crack" that could be heard by those in the upper deck, a Cinderella story ended like *Nightmare on Elm Street*.

In the weeks that followed, the decisions were agonizing. The prayers, real. The surgery, radical. And while the doctors assured him that the cancer was gone, so was his arm. And not just part of his arm, but the entire arm and most of his shoulder.

There were many difficult first steps that Dave had to take following his surgery:

The first time he forced himself to stand in front of the mirror and look at the hole where his arm had been.

The first time of struggling to button a shirt with one hand, of staring at his shoelaces and wondering how in the world he would tie them, of feeling the phantom pains in his fingertips—when there's no hand there to feel.

We had the privilege of sharing dinner with our friend Dave Dravecky and his exceptional wife, Jan, on the eve of another first. The next morning he was to face a hoard of anxious TV talk show hosts and newspaper reporters who had descended on Orlando for his first public interview since the operation.

Facing live cameras and national media attention is something Dave learned to take in stride in his years as a baseball star. The interview would go incredibly well. His words shared with millions of viewers were a crystal-clear testimony of his undaunted courage and his unshaken personal faith in Jesus Christ. But the night before, at an intimate dinner, we got to hear about an even more touching first.

The difficulty he faced when his two children saw him for the first time with no arm.

THE DAY DADDY CAME HOME

Dave and Jan had decided not to have the kids come to the hospital during the short time he was recuperating. Instead, the day Dave came home, he called each child into the room, one by one, to see their daddy.

His son, Mike, was the first to come in. An energetic nine-year-old who loves baseball and his father, he walked all around the room, looking at Dad from all angles.

Finally, Dave said to him, "Well . . . do you want to see my scar?"

"Yea!" his son said, his eyes lighting up.

Carefully removing the bandages, he showed Mike the massive job of suturing that had been done following surgery.

"Gosh, Dad," he said. "Wait right here. I'll be right back, I promise. Don't go anywhere." Many minutes went by before Mike came back into the room.

"Dad, I've got some of my friends outside. Can they come in and see your scar?" Any doubts Dave might have had about his son being distant or uncomfortable around him were dispelled as he became the best "show and tell" object on the block. Young boys take to scars like a badge of courage. But what would happen with his daughter? Would an empty sleeve put a barrier between him and his daughter?

Anna, his precious seven-year-old, had waited patiently outside for her turn to see Daddy. When it finally came, she ran to him. And when she reached him, he was able to do something he hadn't done for months while his painfully cancerous arm was in a sling—give her a big hug.

"Well . . . what do you think?" he asked her, with a smile.

"Daddy," she said, "I'm glad they took your arm off."

"You are?" he asked, taken slightly off guard. "How come?"

"Because now you can hug me again!"

As traumatic as it was in many ways, Dave Dravecky wasn't broken by what happened to him. Shaken, set back, honest about his struggles, but not shattered.

As a baseball player, he'd never climb a mound again, put his rally cap on backwards in the bull pen, or get another strikeout to go on the back of a baseball card. In an instant, his professional power dropped totally out of the box scores. But that didn't finish Dave Dravecky; it just moved him into a different league.

In the Official Scorer's Book of Life—the one that scores each of us daily as a husband, a father, and a godly man—he went five-for-five and pitched a shutout game, when it came to using his personal power for good. And what this man pictures to perfection is something each one of us needs to perfect.

THERE ARE ONLY TWO CHOICES ON HOW WE'LL FACE THE FUTURE

As important as it is to deal with our past, it's equally important that we have a clear plan for our future. And while we may not realize it, each of us chooses from one of two inner road maps as we steer towards what's to come.

These two road maps involve choices we make about the future. And the outcome of our choices will radically affect the way we treat others, how highly we value ourselves, and even our personal health!

What are our options?

We've already seen one. Dave Dravecky illustrates one choice we can make—the ability to confidently and positively face the future.

What comes from the Dravecky school of facing the future? Try an honest optimism that leads to action, not denial. It spurs a man to make a clear plan, keeps a tremendous, life-long challenge before him, and draws out his best efforts at commitment and self-control. But it's not our only option.

For many of us, we'll make a choice to view what's ahead of us in a way that guarantees us a losing season. And it's usually decided when we wait until we get a wake-up call from life before facing our future. Consider these examples:

The sixty-four-year-old major airline captain suddenly realizes his scheduling supervisor is counting down the flights until he is forced to retire.

The rumor that "a number of long-term employees" are being laid off shoots through the department so fast, even a Star Wars defense couldn't stop it.

A young man's parents notify him that after graduation, his subsidized lifestyle is going to change radically.

The ultrasound confirms that it's not twins in six months, but triplets!

When we can't avoid facing the future, too many of us swerve away from learned hopefulness and crash headlong into a self-erected barrier called learned helplessness.

What is this second option when it comes to facing our future? See if you can identify it in the story that follows.

I'm thirty-four years old, and I've been married three times. (Not my fault; I always seem to pick losers.) My problem is my hair...or lack of it.

I know that many men feel there's nothing wrong with being bald, but I do. I started losing my hair when I was in high school and have tried everything I know since to stop what's happening to me or reverse it.

I know that my first wife left me because of my hair. My latest wife even told me straight out that I was obsessed with my hair and that was why she was leaving.

My lack of hair is ruining my life! I know it's the reason I'm not making sales like I used to. I can tell that people look at me differently.

When I was eighteen, I had hair implants put in, and then again at twenty-one. I even went to a well-known plastic surgeon recently and offered to pay him in advance for transplanting whatever skin I needed to fix my head.

All he did was insult me by saying that I shouldn't waste my money on scalp surgery. The money I spend on my head should be spent to see a psychiatrist!

I'm sure that doctor wasn't a Christian. That's why I'm writing you to ask your advice.

When it comes to facing the future, this man has a major problem. In his mind (or actually on top of his mind), there's something that will forever keep him from finishing first in life—or even coming in a strong second.

He can't picture a successful future for himself without thick, curly locks of hair. And by picking out something in his life he is powerless to change and making it the source of all his problems, he is directly affecting his entire future.

What this man has chosen, as have many people like him, is a life based on *learned helplessness*. Learned helplessness comes when we convince ourselves that we're missing something in the present that holds the key to our future. Usually, there's some trauma or event in the past that convinces us fate has already dealt us a losing hand, and we're powerless to draw any more cards.

How common is this problem for men?

Epidemic.

Now, usually it's not something as noticeably vain as a preoccupation with hair. For most men, the difference between a good haircut and a bad one is about a week. Most of us are thankful for whatever hair we have left and whatever color it's becoming.

But take a long look in the mirror and ask yourself if you've defined your future around any of the following:

> "If I would have married _____, things would have been different . . ."
> "If I had chosen college instead of my trade, I wouldn't be in the situation I'm in now . . ."
> "If my parents would have stayed together . . ."
> "If my pastor hadn't fallen . . ."
> "If my coach would have just played me . . ."
> "If my company hadn't transferred me . . ."
> "If my father would have given me the breaks he gave my brother . . ."

LEARNED HELPLESSNESS: FOLLOWING A ROAD MAP TO DISASTER

Learned helplessness is just what this title spells out. It's a practiced way of viewing the future that keeps us dependent on the past. And it can strike a devastating blow to our sense of self-worth and, in turn, to all our most meaningful relationships.

If we actually "learn" how to be helpless, how do we do so? What starts us down this increasingly bumpy road? In most cases it begins when we see ourselves as "victims."

"When there's no hope of escape..."

Nearly twenty years ago, at the University of Pennsylvania, a surprising observation was made concerning animals. It came from a study that would have animal rights activists today up in arms.

For several months, they placed different dogs in what came to be called a "shuttle box." It was a long, narrow wooden box with a wire grill floor that was divided into two compartments.

A dog was placed in the first section of the box and then received a painful, but not harmful shock. By jumping over the small barrier to the other section of the box, the animal could escape the shock.

As you might expect, the dogs in the study learned very quickly to jump over the barrier and avoid the shock! Small dogs, large dogs, even cats and mice, all reacted the same when put in the shuttle box. When a painful problem (the shock) presented itself, they took action to change their situation and move away from it—quickly! But then one day, this "successful" experiment came to a screeching halt.

In another unrelated experiment, a group of dogs were bound fast in body harnesses. Totally unable to move, they were delivered sixty-four five-second shocks over sixty minutes. Their responses were recorded and the "experiment" concluded. The next day these same dogs were put in the "shuttle box" experiment.

The shock came on, and while all the dogs before them had jumped, these dogs did nothing. Instead of jumping over the small barrier in front of them like all the other animals, they hunkered down, sat still, and endured the pain.

After repeated shocks, an animal might wander across the barrier, ending the shocks. But he didn't learn anything by it. The next time he was put in the box, he would again sit without moving.

A normal dog would whine, bark, or in other ways vent its displeasure. What's more, it would actively make some movement to avoid the shock. But these animals did not. They were passive, almost stoic in the way they sat and endured pain.

Physically, the animals had not been harmed. They were fully capable of taking action to escape the pain. But mentally, that small barrier between them and freedom became Mount Everest.

What were the conclusions drawn from these and a number of other related studies? Namely, that uncontrollable negative experiences can freeze up an animal on the inside, making him passive, pessimistic, and withdrawn.

We know that there is a real danger in jumping from observations of animals to the exceedingly more complex reasoning of humans. But the comparisons are striking.

Experiencing a major trauma—from losing our spouse, to losing our job, to losing our parent's blessing—affects us deeply. But for some of us, it not only marks our past, it immobilizes us as we face the future. Instead of actively trying to solve our problems, we can become passive, dependent, and depressed. In short, we learn that in the face of pain, escape is hopeless. And what's more, we internalize three terrible perspectives on our future.

Our Efforts Won't Match Our Achievement
First, there is the feeling that no matter what we do, our efforts won't match our achievement. The nagging feeling grows that no matter how hard we try, no matter how diligent we become, life won't reward us. Unfortunately, in our fallen world, sometimes this is true. Take Mike for example.

For five years, he worked his way up from bagging groceries to ordering them as assistant manager. Long hours, countless weekends, unquestioned overtime, and accurate accounting at closing. If anyone deserved the promotion to store manager at the new "mega" store about to open, it was Mike. And that's just what he was verbally promised.

Mike's diligent work stood out to be counted, but he never counted on what happened. The absentee owner decided his nephew was cut out for leadership. And with no notice to Mike's superiors, and no experience on the nephew's part, an unqualified man was given the position.

What about Mike? He was given the great opportunity to move to the new store and train the man who sat in the glass office where he should have sat.

That was nine years ago, and Mike has never been the same since. After two bitter years of enduring emotional pain every day, he left the grocery business for an unsuccessful run at college. After failing at that—and his marriage—his life slowed down to a crawl. He's in construction now, but every rent payment is a struggle, and every suggestion to open a door of change is slammed shut.

Why try? is Mike's attitude. After all, it's the "breaks" that make you, not back-breaking work.

Lesson number one, when it comes to learned helplessness is that effort doesn't equal achievement. And there's enough truth in our fallen world to make some of us accept it as absolute fact. For example, in the much-watched world of sports, we consistently hear the comparison of two catches.

Jackie Smith was an NFL tight-end who was ranked with the best in the league for fourteen years. Eight times All-Pro, he was the career reception leader for the Cardinals before he was traded. His efforts over more than a decade inched him towards the Hall of Fame...until one play was run.

It is Superbowl Sunday, January 1973, and his new team, the Dallas Cowboys, is marching for the winning touchdown against the San Francisco 49ers. With his patented moves, Jackie Smith breaks free from the coverage and stands wide open in the end zone.

Danny White, the Cowboys' quarterback, throws a soft spiral that heads right toward Jackie's numbers—and those patented hands. But instead of a vacuum cleaner like they'd been for years, his hands become boards.

The ball bounces off his hands onto the carpet, and the Cowboys lose their chance to score, and the game. Fourteen years, miles of receptions, a room full of awards, and one droped ball.

On a radio talk show, nearly twenty years after that game, Jackie Smith was still having to defend what happened on that one play . . . not receiving praise for all his years of achievement.

Yet another receiver, an overachiever named Phil McConkey,

played only four seasons (three as a back-up) with the New York Giants. But he had one terrific game—in the Superbowl. And made one spectacular catch.

What about Phil? Front cover notice on *Sports Illustrated* and lasting adulation even today from the fans for whom "the catch" was key to a Superbowl win for his team.

In many cases, effort isn't rewarded on an outward basis in our society as much as achievement. But taking a shortcut to fame or fortune (or a degree or position) doesn't carve out the inner depth and maturity that consistency does.

While both carry those two letters behind their name—M.D.— there is a huge difference between the head surgeon at the hospital who has done 500 heart surgeries and the newly graduated medical student who's assisted on five.

Would you stay on a plane if the stewardess announced as you taxied away from the gate, "Serving you today is Captain Johnson. Now this is his first flight, and he's never actually landed a plane this size. But he's sure he can get us off the ground and before we land he'll have plenty of time to read all the manuals . . ."?

Effort does bring inner rewards, if not outward recognition of achievement. Unfortunately, the pain of not seeing our efforts rewarded can convince us that it's pure chance that counts, not persistence. If that's the case, what's the use of genuine effort?

If not seeing effort bring achievement is one step down the road of learned helplessness, it's but a short step to the next...

The Key to Happiness Is Out of Reach
The man lost on the road to learned helplessness often feels that not only does fate rule us, but it's a cruel fate that puts the single key we need to be happy just out of reach.

Take Brian for example. He was the older brother. If Dad should have bonded with anyone, it should have been him! Not his younger brother. He wore his heart out to please his father. But no matter how far he stretched toward him, it seemed he could never reach the arms of acceptance he wanted so much.

In a climate of unfair comparison and favoritism, Brian made a subtle, but terribly damaging decision. Deep inside, he equated what he was missing with what he could never become...younger.

And because he focused on something that could never happen as his key to happiness in the future, it pushed him to committed pessimism . . . and eventually right into clinical depression!

In studies, pessimists persistently look backwards. (For example, pessimists consistently grow up wanting to be younger...optimists grow up looking forward and wishing they were older!) By never being able to "forget what lies behind," they stay stuck in their pain, rather than "pushing forward" to a positive future.

If we feel today's effort doesn't affect our future, and if the only key to change is forever out of our reach, then there's a third trail we can follow right into another lie...

I'm All Alone in My Pain
During the experiments that first showed learned helplessness, the dogs who had experienced the repeated shocks were verbally, even physically, encouraged to jump the barrier, but they didn't. While the shock was going on, it was like the dogs drew so far into an inner, protective shell that they were oblivious to outside encouragement.

Many times we have seen this same type of behavior in men we've counseled! Take Jim, for example. Jim grew up on an Indian reservation, where his father pastored a mission church. When it came to discipline, his father wasn't just strict...he was severe. When Jim was nine years old, he was sitting next to one of his friends at the back of the church, and they whispered about something they were going to do after services.

In the middle of the sermon, suddenly his father's voice rang out Jim's name, ordering him to come up front. Before the entire congregation, Jim's father laid into Jim about how disrespectful and dishonoring he was being in church. And then he took Jim outside (but in full view of the congregation from the windows) and gave him a whipping he's never forgotten.

Many years later, when Jim's marriage began crumbling, his current pain called forth echoes from the past. And wrapped in the powerlessness he felt as a child, he became almost comatose when it came to listening to his wife's complaints or to counsel.

Many men who have gone through some kind of trauma see a painful situation coming and beat a hasty, inner retreat. Instead of being open to counsel, or hearing another cry for help, they pull further and further inside. They isolate themselves more and more, cutting themselves off from genuine help and a brighter future.

If our efforts don't count, and the key to change is out of reach, then a deep sense of impenetrable loneliness sets in. And if we continue to stumble down the road of inner loneliness, we're on our way to disaster. Whether we realize it or not, we share this road with compulsive gamblers, sexaholics, alcoholics, and child abusers who all have something in common: unending loneliness!

Convinced deep inside that there is no escape, this man abuses a drug or his positional power to somehow deaden the pain. But this only compounds the pain in the process, getting him further mired in problems as a result.

The book of Proverbs has much to say about the "sluggard" and the "fool," both models of learned helplessness. Just two of the verses show the foolishness of inner isolation: "He who separates himself [from God and others] is foolish, and quarrels against all sound wisdom." And the final results of having no future: "The sluggard buries his hand in the dish; he will not even bring it back to his mouth" (Proverbs 19:24).

Have you given over your future to some unpredictable "fate," rather than to consistent effort? Does some missing "key" keep the door to change locked in your life? Are you hard of hearing when it comes to accepting, even asking for, sound counsel?

Then you're right where the enemy wants you. Following a road map to dead-end relationships and an unfulfilled life.

But there's hope. Promise yourself and your future that you'll seek inner change, seek wise counsel, and avoid learned helplessness. Some of the wise counsel that you may be desiring can be found in the following articles. Listen with your soul and ask God to help you keep these important promises to the future. Remember, your past does not have to bind your future. As the apostle Paul wrote, "Forgetting what is behind and straining toward what is ahead, I press on toward the goal to win the prize for which God has called me heavenward in Christ Jesus" (Philippians 3:13-14).

The Right Choice

Dennis Rainey

Driving home last night after work I switched on the radio to catch the news. In a moment of uncharacteristic sincerity, the announcer made a statement that sliced through my fog of fatigue:

"I hope you did something of value today. You wasted a whole day if you didn't."

His statement struck me abruptly. Fortunately, I felt pretty good about how I had invested my time that day solving some of the problems of a swiftly growing organization. But in ten minutes I would be home where one lovely lady and six pairs of little feet would want and need my attention.

Would I do something of value with them tonight?

"It's just one night," I thought. "And besides, I'm exhausted." Then I pondered how one night followed by another, 365 times, adds up to a year. The nights and years seemed to be passing with increasing velocity. I thought of our two oldest children, who in only a couple of years will both be drafted into the war of adolescence.

"I hope you did something of value today. You wasted a whole day if you didn't." Those words echoed in my thoughts as I drove through the darkness. Five minutes more, and I'd be home.

"I'll bet I do better than average with my kids," I thought. But then another question came to mind: Did God call me to be merely a better-than-average husband and father?

It's just one night. One night. What will I accomplish? Will I waste it spending all evening in front of the television? Or invest it in planting the seeds of a positive legacy for my children?

I wanted just one evening of selfishness—to do my own thing. But what if Barbara felt the same way?

What kind of heritage and legacy will I impart? Selfishness? Or selflessness? One more minute, and I'd be home.

"Just one night, Lord. It's just one night." But then the same angel who wrestled Jacob to the ground pinned me with a half-nelson as I drove into the garage. Okay, I give in. You've got me.

As the kids surrounded my car like a band of whooping Indians, screaming, "Daddy, Daddy, Daddy," I was glad on this night I had made the right choice.

At supper, rather than just grazing our way through the groceries, we spent a few moments on nostalgia. Each of us answered the question, What were your favorite things we did as a family this past year?

After supper, I gave the kids three choices of what we would do: Play Monopoly together as a family, read a good book together quietly, or wrestle together on the living room floor. Which do you think they chose?

Three little sumo wrestlers grabbed my legs and began to drag me into the living room. Dad was pinned by the kids. Mom was tickled by Dad. And kids went flying through the air (literally) for the next hour. Even our ten-month-old got in on the act by pouncing on me after she had observed the other kids in action.

Will the kids remember? Maybe, but I doubt it.

Did I waste the evening? No. With God's power, I did my best to leave a legacy that counts—a legacy that will outlive me.

I was reminded of two things. First, I remember what Paul wrote in Ephesians 5:15-17(NASB): "Therefore be careful how you walk, not as unwise men, but as wise, making the most of your time, because the days are evil. So then do not be foolish, but understand what the will of the Lord is."

Second, I remembered my dad. He was badgered by one determined boy into playing catch over and over again. I can still remember his well-worn mitt and curve ball.

If you struggle as I do with priorities, you might want to commit to memory those verses in Ephesians. The "fool" Paul wrote about is someone we never intend to become. It "just happens."

We Need Visionaries

Bill Hybels

Vision is on my endangered character quality list along with courage and discipline. The reason is simple: It takes too much work to be a visionary. It's much easier just to go with the flow and do what's expected. It takes courage to break out of conventional thought patterns. It takes confidence and daring to risk failure with a new idea or a new approach. Visionaries tend to fail many times before they ever succeed, and most people feel too fragile to take risks. They would rather be safe and secure.

It also takes a lot of old-fashioned perspiration to be a visionary. It takes discipline to sit down with a pencil and paper and vow not to get up from your desk until you find five new ways to do something, three new ways to improve something, or two new options for salvaging something that is in danger of disintegrating. It takes endurance to get on your knees and stay there until God supernaturally ignites a fresh thought in your mind. It takes hard work to plan for what could happen in six months, a year, three years, or five years in your business, family, marriage, or ministry. It probably won't ever happen anyway, so why dream?

Many of us seem to think that dreams, grandiose plans, and creative bursts are reserved for writers, physicists, composers, and artists. They are not for ordinary people with ordinary vocations, ordinary families, and ordinary relationships. But I think God disagrees with that kind of thinking. I think He would say that vision, like courage and discipline, is a character trait that can be stimulated and developed in anyone who is willing to understand what it is and then to work hard at making it a part of everyday life.

History Is Alive

Udo Middelman

M y children have often tried to be a part of my childhood. "Where was I when you were in school, Daddy?" "Tell me some naughty things you did when you were young, please."

Visits to museums, walking on Roman roads in Europe, explaining the Greek architecture of some American government buildings, explaining why the Christian churches are found in the center of old towns, are all links with our past. The human race does not start with me or my parents. We have a history of greatness and foolishness. It has shaped us and the world we live in.

History gives continuity. It confirms a needed stability. There are explanations for us and our lives. We have a name, for we are part of the human race. People like us did not just appear yesterday—or by chance. We even have a family name; we are children of our father and mother. We should find out who they are.

Without a history a people does not have a future. Sadly too many broken families destroy the knowledge of personal history. Looking ahead only, wishing for a better tomorrow, is like a tree without roots, a building without foundations.

A life anchored in the soil of history looks back to struggle and achievement. Individuals with names have made history. Their efforts have found some reward. Their hopes were often realized, but not without effort, study, overcoming failure, sometimes even being despised.

Our present culture has turned history into anecdotes, not the struggle of human beings with basic issues of life and death, right and wrong. We are told to look ahead, as if things will just work out and happiness will never end. With these expectations, we also smash the history of our relationships, our marriages, our culture. We move often, tearing at the foundations. We assume the ideal is around the next turn, but we forget the limits of the real world, real history, our history.

We are not at the beginning. God is Creator and eyewitness of it. He tells us what went ahead of us. He sets the history we must continue. Without it we will scatter, becoming as confused as many a child today who does not know his father or mother, without lasting relations, no place to call home, facing a random future without a solid past.

Think for a moment of how many future perspectives have surfaced in our time and then went out like a light after destroying numerous lives. Paul Johnson mentions Marx, Freud, and the popular interpretation of Einstein having fathered programs that advocate a new humanity. Marxism, fascism, the sexual revolution, and moral relativism have all imposed their cruel toll on people who only wanted a break with the past. What was new turned out to be the systematic killing of people, their bodies, hearts and minds. Though those movements suggested a new humanitarian impulse, individuals by the thousands were sacrificed in pursuit of what was billed as historic change. But it was an appeal to a fantasy, not to real history. For many that insight comes too late.

To give shape to the future, and to work within true boundaries, we need to discover and talk about real history that stretches to the beginning. Eusebius, Thomas Aquinas, Martin Luther, the Founding Fathers are a part of that history. Byzantine mosaics, Michelangelo, Bach and the traders of Venice, Amsterdam and Novgorod have retained our understanding of the sanctity of the life of men and women. But behind this is the God of the Bible, who alone affirms His image in each person. He, not chance or the unknown, no impersonal primal soup, gives us a name: man. He tells us of the Fall in history, when things fell apart to leave us broken, fragile, and outside of his garden. The Bible tells us about God's love for His creatures, His running after them to repurchase them in history. Only this way, and in contrast to ancient and modern myths around the world, are we at home, not orphans lost in the cosmos. Without it we are strangers in a world of wild things.

The denial of this history, making it merely stories of primitive ancestors with a religious bent, has led to the primitive cruelty of political, intellectual, emotional, and economic murder of our own century. We have become the primitives, for we hope that the future will be better, when only the past can give us direction, explanation, and limitations.

People who played god by giving new definitions in our century acted like devils. Our children will hold our feet to the fire, until we can explain to them who we are, to what family of man we belong.

Ignoring Warning Signals

Jay Carty

I have a friend who was a fighter pilot in World War II. During his training, he flew planes that didn't have radios. That's the way it was in those days. Signal men on the ground communicated with the young flyers by waving flags.

Bill was the best in his class and had a chance to prove it during the graduation exercises. With the grandstands full of top brass, sweet William set out to make a mark for himself. He won the touch-and-go competition easily, captured first place in the dog fight event, and thereby won the right to land first.

Bill was feeling fine. Top Gun, that's who he was. And he was leading the parade. As he was enjoying his victory, he thought of making a perfect landing just to cap off a perfect day of flying. He thought about the applause awaiting him as he climbed out of his plane.

My friend lowered his flaps as he started his approach. A buzzer went off in the cockpit. Bill knew what it meant but was so caught up in the moment that it didn't register. He could see the men in the tower waving with both hands. "Hi, guys," he yelled knowing they couldn't hear him. How nice of them to welcome the conquering hero. Then a red flare sailed across his vision. Fireworks for the winner. They had thought of everything.

Concentrate, concentrate. Focus on making both wheels touch at the same time.

As the plane settled to the ground Bill noticed the propeller stop. This phenomenon was followed by the screech of metal. The propeller had stopped because it had hit the ground. The ear piercing sound was caused by the body of the plane doing the same thing. As a cloud of dust enveloped the plane, Bill remembered, "I forgot to put down the landing gear; I didn't lower the wheels!"

Bill thought he was a winner. He thought everything was just fine...until it was too late.

Oh, he'd been warned. The buzzer was installed as a reminder to the pilot to put his gear down when the flaps were lowered. The guys in the tower tried to wave him off. The red flare was an attempt to keep him from landing.

But Bill crashed. And now it was too late. Nothing more could be done. This book is a friend in the tower trying to wave you off. It's a final flare. It just might be your last warning buzzer. Get your wheels down. Don't crash.

Back to the Real Future

Fran Sciacca

A n MBA, a BMW, and a condo in Vail." I had asked my high school seniors what they wanted for their lives. This response came from a stable, morally sound kid. He, like his peers, has been coached to do well in school so he can compete in the marketplace, secure a good job and provide for his family. I have no doubt that his parents believe they have been faithful to their Christian calling. Sadly, however, they have missed a more important future that their son needs to prepare for—Heaven.

The future for the committed Christian of the twenty-first century must be defined within a biblical circumference. It is not just jobs, homes, children, and financial security for retirement. The real future for the child of God is the life that begins when this one ends.

To prepare our children, we men must teach them to live now in light of eternity. But we may first have to change how we see ourselves in relation to God and the world around us. This may necessitate serious spiritual heart surgery for us fathers. We need to look deep inside and find out what our own hearts beat for— because our children already know, even if we don't.

The Scriptures speak of two classes of people: those who are "of the world" and those who are not:

> "If you belonged to the world, it would love you as its own. As it is, you do not belong to the world, but I have chosen you out of the world. That is why the world hates you." (John 15:19)

The Bible has a sobering description of a follower of Christ; one that flies in the face of being permanent residents here on earth. It is that of an alien or stranger. The heroes of the faith from the beginning of time were described in Hebrews 11:13:

All these people were still living by faith when they died. They did not receive the things promised; they only saw them and welcomed them from a distance. And they admitted that they were aliens and strangers on earth.

Peter and Paul both subscribe to this alien description of the believer as well:

Dear friends, I urge you, as aliens and strangers in the world. (1 Peter 2:11)

But our citizenship is in heaven. And we eagerly await a Savior from there, the Lord Jesus Christ. (Philippians 3:20)

"Alien" and "stranger" have the combined meaning of someone who is "staying for a while in a strange place." We are an outpost of Heaven here on earth. The bumper sticker "Just Visiting This Planet" is profoundly true!

Earth is our present domicile, but it is not our home. There will come a day at a point in history when we will exit this life and become permanent residents in the presence of God. Do you live in light of that fact?

I find increasingly that my students are focused on a future defined by this world of space and time. Fathers, is it possible that we are training our children to be "tourists" rather than aliens?

Tourists are aliens without allegiance. They look for pleasure, not purpose. Tourists love the world, but are indifferent to the people of it. And, tragically, tourists are often offensive and rude to the real residents.

Scripture is clear—our goal is to enlarge the Kingdom of God (Matthew 8:19-20). What we owe the future, then, is to instill in our families the notion that we are aliens here, not tourists. We need to value supremely the one thing that God values—people.

Our children must see in our lives and hear from our lips that people are more important to us than our things, their things, and the world's things. How do you respond when your new car gets its first dent? Do you keep upgrading your home and possessions? Do you seek to increase your leisure life or do you share your extra time and prosperity with people? Do your children hear your concern and prayer that unbelieving coworkers would come to Christ? Does your boss, or your employee, wonder why you're so different? In short, is there an alien character about you?

We need to plan for college, career, and family. But we need to be most prepared for the future that begins when this life ends. As promise keepers we should be committed to the truth that we are just passing through planet earth. Ask your family what they think you live for—then prepare your heart to become an alien.

13

Practicing Learned Hopefulness

Gary Smalley and John Trent

Two years in solitary confinement. Leg irons shackled around your ankles fifteen hours a day. No light in your cell, except for that one single bulb that comes on at dark and stays on until daybreak.

After over 300 brutal interrogations, having your already broken leg deliberately snapped, being beaten in the face with a fan belt until you go into convulsions, repeatedly being shown pictures of Jane Fonda leading protests back home while denied letters from your wife . . . you're only halfway through your 2,714 days in captivity.

If anyone should have been a candidate for learned helplessness, it was Captain James Stockdale. Yet as the senior American officer at the infamous "Hanoi Hilton," he never gave up and never gave in to the enemy's demands that he be used for propaganda.

In the hands of his brutally cruel North Vietnamese captors, he had no positional power whatsoever. But he maintained—actually increased—his personal power to the point that it was unbreakable.

"Over my dead body will I be used. Over my dead body will I let my fellow prisoners down . . ."

In even the most painful past or present situation, there is still a choice we face. Even if we're helpless to change our circumstances, we can still choose to make inner alterations to our character. And one of the most important ways to multiply our personal power as a man is to practice a view of the future we call *learned hopefulness*.

FOURTH DOWN, AND A FUTURE TO GO

Middle linebackers have a look about them. Maybe it's their eyes that are always darting back and forth, their inner intensity, or their ability to intimidate everyone—including the waitress that hustles to bring coffee.

For seven years after playing at the University of Nebraska, Monte Johnson had been at the center of an Oakland Raider defense—a black-clad, punishing defense that had taken them to the playoffs and pounded opponents each Sunday. Monte was as powerful as they come on the playing field. But on one play during the preseason following their Superbowl win, Monte's playing career was shattered, and for the first time he seemed powerless to change his situation.

When we met at a pro athletes conference, he was recuperating from knee surgery, and facing the most difficult time in his life. In a few weeks, he had to report back to his team for preseason training, and with the injury, a very real possibility of being cut.

The thought of his livelihood instantly gone and his options uncertain, he turned his frustration inward, fighting a losing season within himself.

That's when we had a long talk, and I (Gary) shared with him much of what we'd like to share with you now. In the last chapter, we looked at how learned helplessness follows three downward steps. Like its twisted counterpart, learned hopefulness is also built upon three important steps. Only these three uplifting steps can spell the beginning of a special future . . . even if we're at the end of the line. These three uplifting steps can help you become a man who keeps his promises, a man who can choose a promising future.

Learned Hopefulness Starts with Commitment

That day, as I sat for hours talking with Monte, three things stood out in our conversation. Actually, all three of them were steps he had taken to become a success in his sport, and now those same qualities would hold the key to a future full of potential.

As we talked, one thing quickly became obvious. Years before, Monte had made a commitment that he was going to be an outstanding football player. It was that commitment that took him through the two-a-days during training camp, the unreasonable coaches, and the crushing defeats.

It's Maintained Through Self-Control

Once Monte made the commitment to become a football star, he linked it with tremendous self-control. While others were getting summer jobs as lifeguards around the pool, he was driving steel on a work crew. When the average person still had his head on the pillow, he was pounding the pavement and running wind-sprints. Because of his commitment, he was willing to make sacrifices, all because they pointed toward an ultimate end.

It Centers Around a Significant Challenge

Each season in the pros, there was a clear-cut challenge put before Monte: to be the best at his position and to help his team get to the world championship. With twenty-six teams and a league full of talent, that was not a minor challenge, but an enormous one. And for year after year, those three factors of commitment, self-control, and a clear challenge gave him a reason to face the future! Interestingly, as we talked, all three qualities had been lost in one play when his knee was blown out.

Actually, those important habits of the heart hadn't been lost, just moved out of sight. For as Monte and I talked that day, it was like a barrier lifted, and he saw again what it would take, outside of football, to win in each season of life.

What Monte learned that day is what we want to share with you as well—namely, the three steps that lead to learned hopefulness which lie at the heart of our personal power. They are the keys to keeping the promises we've examined in this book.

Commitment

If your future seems bleak, then the first thing to do is reexamine your commitments. Monte Johnson was already a Christian, and right there we started as I asked him three questions.

"Do you want your life to count for Jesus Christ?" I asked him.

"Absolutely," he said.

No matter what changes in our circumstances, our commitment

to Christ can be that one anchor in the storm. And because He can be our solid rock, we may be lashed by the storm, but we will not washed away.

"Do you want to be the husband and father God would have you be?" I asked.

Again, the answer was a resounding "yes."

John and I team-teach a conference all across the country called the "Love Is a Decision" seminar. And the name is there for a reason. One of the greatest strengths of a man is that he can make a decision to love . . . independent from his feelings.

And finally, I asked Monte, "Are you willing to do whatever it takes to be the man He wants you to be?"

"Sure . . . but I don't know who He wants me to be now that I'm not a football player!" he answered.

A key to sorting out the confusion comes first with the commitment we make to Christ, then to our family and finally to growing as a person. Then once our commitment is reaffirmed, it's backed up with:

Self-Control

As we counsel men, one glaring problem that surfaces is a lack of self-control. And not surprisingly, the degree of self-control an person has is in direct proportion to his self-worth.

In a previous chapter we spoke about the need to "pull in the reins" on bad habits and how a lack of self-worth contributes to this problem.

In times of transition, we often lose the emotional energy to discipline our attitudes and appetites. We "reward" ourselves with junk food instead of exercise, let five hours a night go by before we finally turn off the television, and procrastinate on what we need to do at work, while doing only what we like to do. And in large part, that is because we're missing a third key element to a successful future:

A Clear Challenge

Don had built his life around his family. All three boys had been athletes, both in high school and college. He had coached their little league teams. Then in the changeable Seattle weather, he had watched every game and many practices as the years went by. He was as supportive as a father could be . . . and as lost as a man could be when his sons outgrew sports.

In tears he admitted to his middle son, "I have to find a purpose beyond you boys. I've been so wrapped up in your sports, I've lost any other direction."

The fact is, many men get so wrapped up in a time-limited challenge, that it can actually kill them! It's a fact that the average man dies within a few years of retirement. This isn't an argument against retirement homes. Actually, it's a reflection of a crisis most men face. For many men the challenge of work keeps them going. But when that challenge is no longer before them, they don't know who they are. And that nagging sense of uselessness and purposelessness proves fatal to many systems.

How clear is your purpose in life? Do you have a challenge in life that is bigger than your job? Or one that can motivate you if you're in a "bad" job or have no job at all? You can if you put these three elements of a special future into practice. And one specific way to do that is to keep before you what we call the "5 M's."

As Monte and I talked that day, I wrote down five things that I felt were crucial for him to consider:

- Master
- Mate
- Mission
- Method
- Maintenance

The first thing Monte had to be clear on was who his Master was and what his commitment was to Him. As we'll see later, we will never have the inner power to deal with problems, challenges, and people in life without making clear our relationship to our Master.

Next comes our mate. For many men, they jump past this second step to the third. "What I do" becomes more important than "who I am related to." However, public success is shallow at best without private victory at home. Understanding the basic needs of your wife and children are requirements, not electives, as we face the future.

The security of being committed to Christ and the support that comes from a well-loved family lead us to talk about a third critical choice in becoming a promise keeper. This is an area that took Monte and I several hours to pound out, and it may take you even longer. Monte came up with a clear mission he could use to provide the challenge he needed as a man.

We talked about Monte's strengths as a person, what gave him the most fulfillment in life, what he missed doing. Interestingly, all the feedback I received had to do with solving problems! Math was his favorite subject in school. Calling the signals on defense became a problem-solving exercise. Even helping his children work through problems they faced gave him great joy.

Was helping people "solve problems" a big enough goal to last a lifetime? With all the mistakes people were making around us, it certainly seemed like something with a future! But how, specifically, could he help others?

With his Master, mate, and mission now in clear focus, there were a thousand possible methods he could use to accomplish his task. But as we talked further about what problems most distressed him, and which he'd most like to solve, one opportunity stood out—helping people with financial difficulties.

There seem to be enough people struggling in this area to command Monte's attention until Jesus returns! And while it may not seem possible considering the inflated salaries many proathletes receive, Monte had seen many of them end their careers bankrupt and in bondage to debt.

The more we talked, the more excited he became that he could begin to make a difference in people's lives who were hurting financially. Think of the freedom it would give them, the reduction of stress in their marriages, the helpful legacy they could leave to their children, the ministries that could be funded through proper stewardship!

The more we talked, the more excited we both became as we pictured him as a financial counselor, a tremendous resource to God's people! But then we hit a potential problem—Monte had no formal training as a financial counselor!

Here's where many people get bogged down. They make the commitment to go for the best in their relationship with Christ, their Master, and their mate and family. They even isolate a challenging personal mission and pinpoint a primary method to accomplish it. But then they let the "realities" of additional schooling or training derail the dream.

As Monte and I talked further, we saw that even though his formal education and former vocation hadn't directly prepared him for his mission, they had given him indirect advantages. The hours of discipline on the practice field all stressed "doing things right" in the game; the college courses in communication he took would help him get a financial point across to a couple or group. Even his summer jobs of laying steel stressed the need to build a solid foundation if a building was to hold together.

Monte went away from our session convinced that he did have a mission to fulfill apart from football. He was confident the method he'd chosen was a sound one. That's when he had such confidence in prayer to commit his upcoming meeting with the Raider's coach.

If he was cut, he now had a lifetime plan to fall back on—one flexible enough to change "methods" a dozen times, but one focused enough to give him an exciting view of the future. And as it turned out, he needed it. He was cut. But instead of blowing up or pointing fingers, Monte did something no player had ever done with his coach. He shook his hand and thanked him for cutting him and for clarifying the direction that God wanted him to go in his life.

Did Monte's story end there? No. For he kept one more "M" before him on a daily basis: maintenance. That meant he was determined to work on whatever schooling it would take and committed each day to bathing in prayer the "mission" and "method" he felt would honor God.

By beginning with the end in mind, it wouldn't make any difference if Monty had to cook pizzas for a short time to keep food on the Johnson's table. In the process of being a pizza cook, he knew now he'd be learning things that could help him as a financial counselor. Whether that involved "coffee cup" counseling with another employee God brought him alongside or learning more about business accounting from the owner.

Suddenly, setbacks and delays were easier to deal with because even in the detours important things could be learned. And the learning didn't happen only at work. With his commitment to Christ and his family as first priorities in his plan, he was very aware that to teach financial wisdom and restraint, he had to be living it at home. What's more, he needed to teach it first to his children successfully before he exported it.

Commitment, self-control, a significant challenge. The very things every man needs were what this unemployed, ex-football player had the day he "retired." And these kept him going until several months after his forced retirement from the pros, when the phone rang, and he was offered a position with one of the most influential Christian financial counselors in our country.

Monte's story isn't an exception. It actually points out a rule we all need to follow as men. Namely, as believers we don't have the option set before us to traffic in learned helplessness. We have the opportunity to choose a learned hopefulness and become men who keep our promises.

Look at God's Word as we close this important section, and see what kind of promising future He calls us to:

"Do not let your hearts be troubled. Trust in God; trust also in me. In my Father's house are many rooms; if it were not so, I would have told you. I am going to prepare a place for you. And if I go and prepare a place for you, I will come back and take you to be with me that you also may be where I am. You know the way to the place where I am going." (John 14:1-4)

Take the Road Less Traveled

Bill McCartney

W hen men come together in the name of Jesus Christ, there's a dynamic that takes place. There's an unleashing of God's Spirit that doesn't exist at other times to the same extent.

In recent times two certain men have been in the news. Although these guys have a great deal in common, there's a direct contrast in the way that they express themselves and in the attitudes they have. Let me show you the contradiction. The first man has told us, "I never questioned the reason for my assignment. I saluted smartly and charged up the hill." The second man, after his valiant heroics, said, "If it ever came to a choice between compromising my moral principles in the performance of my duties, I know I'd go with my moral principles."

Do you see the contradiction? Do you see the difference in the attitude? The choices that we make as men really dictate the outcome of our lives. Robert Frost said it this way, "Two roads diverged in the woods . . . I took the one less traveled by." There are two roads out there, men. The Bible is very clear about that. The Bible describes one road as a broad highway that leads to destruction and most men are on that road. But there's a straight and narrow road that leads to life and very few ever find it. Furthermore, there's competition to get us on those roads. One road, the highway, is so alluring, it seems to promise everything. The other road, at first, seems to deny us all the things that we would really enjoy.

The competition to get us on these two roads isn't like an athletic contest. At an athletic contest we know beforehand the designated place and time. Our adversary is identified for us. But in the contest of life, things are different. Our adversary, we're told, sometimes prowls like a roaring lion looking for someone to devour, but other times he masquerades as an angel of light. We don't know when or where he's going to show up next.

So, how do we prepare for this adversary in life? (As I said before, at Colorado we suspect he's going to be wearing Nebraska's colors—red and white.) In this world, he comes in many different shapes and forms. The one thing in our favor is that we know those of us that are on the straight and narrow path that leads to life have an extremely capable leader in Jesus Christ, the King of kings, and the Lord of lords.

You and I serve royalty. And those of us who do serve have a responsibility that's costly. Christ has said, "Whoever serves me must follow me, and where I am my servant also will be." But listen to this promise in John 12:26: "My Father will honor the one who serves me." There isn't anything that I want more in my life than to serve Jesus Christ, because I want Almighty God's favor upon me.

The passion of our lives should be Romans 8:29: "To be conformed to the likeness" of Jesus Christ. That's our purpose and should be our greatest pursuit.

God has promised.

Author Index

Ken Abraham is the author of *Unmasking the Myths of Marriage, This Is Not the Trip I Signed Up For, Positive Holiness, The Disillusioned Christian,* and other titles. He is a highly sought after speaker and lives in Nashville, Tennessee, with his wife and two daughters. His articles appear on pages 56, 128, and 163.

Bob Beltz is a speaker, author, and serves as pastor to Cherry Hills Community Church in Denver, Colorado. His article appears on page 140.

Wellington Boone is the president and founder of New Generation Campus Ministries and understands the inner city because he grew up in an inner-city ghetto in New Jersey. Now married and the father of three children, two of them teenagers, Rev. Boone is currently senior pastor of Manna Christian Fellowship in Richmond, Virginia. His article appears on page 184.

Jerry Bridges is vice-president for corporate affairs of The Navigators. Jerry combines a Bible teaching ministry with his corporate responsibilities for The Navigators. He is the author of *The Pursuit of Holiness, The Practice of Godliness, Trusting God,* and *Transforming Grace.* The article on page 126 is from *The Crisis of Caring* by Jerry Bridges, P&R Publishing. Used by permission of the author.

John E. Brown III is president of John Brown University in Siloam Springs, Arkansas. His articles appear on pages 87 and 168.

Ken Brown has been the associate pastor at Metro Denver Church on the Rock for the past five years. He has been involved in marriage counseling and relationship teaching for twenty-five years and is a popular speaker for marriage seminars. Ken and his wife, Fonda, have four children and reside in Arvada, Colorado. His article is located on page 76.

Steve Brown teaches daily on the "Keylife" radio broadcast over stations in forty-five states and speaks at conferences throughout North America. His latest books are *If Jesus Has Come* and *Jumpings Hurdles, Hitting Glitches, Overcoming Setbacks.* His article appears on page 90.

Harold Bussell is the author of *Lord, I Can Resist Anything But Temptation, Unholy Devotion,* and *Why Christians Are Lured to the Cults.* He is currently serving as senior pastor at the Hamilton Congregational Church in Hamilton, Massachusetts. His articles appear on pages 52 and 110.

Ken R. Canfield is research scholar, founder, and executive director of the Center for Fathering. The articles on pages 98, 108, and 112 are from: *Seven Secrets of Effective Fathers*, by Ken R. Canfield ©1992. Used by permission of Tyndale House Publishers, Inc. All rights reserved.

Jay Carty is the founder and director of YES! Ministries in Corvallis, Oregon. He is the author of *Only Tens Go to Heaven, Counterattack*, and *Something's Fishy*. His articles appear on pages 100, 166, and 220. These articles are reprinted from the book *Something's Fishy* by Jay Carty, copyright 1990 by Jay Carty. Published by Multnomah Press, Portland, Oregon 97266. Used by permission.

Edwin Louis Cole is an author, speaker, and the founder and president of the Christian Men's Network. Cole travels extensively, showing men how to realize their dreams of real manhood by looking to Jesus Christ as their role model. He has an article on page 138, reprinted with permission from *On Becoming a Real Man*, by Edwin Louis Cole, published by Thomas Nelson Publishers.

Dr. Larry Crabb is an author, lecturer, and the founder and director of the Institute of Biblical Counseling. Among his best-selling books are *Inside Out* and *Men & Women*. His article on page 48 was taken from the book, *Men & Women* by Dr. Larry J. Crabb. Copyright © 1990 by Lawrence J. Crabb, Jr. Used by permission.

Gordon Dalbey is a teacher, ordained minister, and author of *Healing the Masculine Soul*. The article on page 122 is from *Healing the Masculine Soul* by Gordon Dalbey, © 1989 published by Word Books, Dallas, Texas.

Steve Diggs is the chairman of The Franklin Group, Inc. The Nashville-based firm has two award-winning divisions: Steve Diggs and Friends Advertising and Bonner Broadcast Jingles. Steve is a public speaker and author. His latest release is *Free to Succeed*, published by Fleming H. Revell. His article is found on page 192.

Dr. James C. Dobson is founder and president of Focus on the Family, a nonprofit organization that produces his nationally syndicated radio program heard daily on more than 1,550 stations. His many best-selling books include *Parenting Isn't for Cowards, Hide or Seek, The Strong-Willed Child, Love Must Be Tough*, and *Love for a Lifetime*.
Dr. Dobson's article appears on page 158 and is reprinted from *Straight Talk* by James C. Dobson, copywritten in 1991 and published by Word Books, Dallas, Texas. It is used with permission.

Steve Farrar speaks to thousands of people each year in evangelical churches across North America. His well-known conference, "Building Strong Families," is recognized as one of the foremost equipping tools for families in the United States today. Steve is president of Strategic Living Ministries in Dallas, Texas. Steve and his wife, Mary, have three children, Rachel, John, and Joshua. The article on page 80 is from the book *Point Man* by Steve Farrar, copyright 1990 by Steve Farrar. Published by Multnomah Press, Portland, Oregon 97266. Used by permission. Another article by Steve is found on page 58.

Leighton Ford, renowned evangelist, has been concentrating on the training of evangelists in all parts of the world. Headquarters for Leighton Ford Ministries is in Charlotte, North Carolina, where his speaking, preaching, and writing ministries are continually in demand. His most recent book is *Jesus the Transforming Leader*. Leighton's article is found on page 17.

Dr. Bill Gaultiere is a licensed psychologist and day hospital director of Minirth-Meier Clinic West in Orange, California. He is the author of *A Walk With Your Shepherd: The Twenty-Third Psalm and the 12 Steps to Recovery*. He holds a master's degree in psychology from Biola University and a Ph.D. in psychology from U.S. International University. He is married, has one son, and lives in Irvine, California. His articles are found on pages 30 and 132.

Dr. Donald R. Harvey, Ph.D., is the clinical director of Christian Counseling Services in Nashville, Tennessee. He is the author of *When the One You Love Wants to Leave, The Drifting Marriage*, and *The Spiritually Intimate Marriage*. His articles are located on pages 74 and 170.

Jack Hayford is the pastor of the Church on the Way in Van Nuys, California. He is also a renowned speaker and author with a special ministry in the area of worship. He article is located on page 149.

Robert Hicks is a counselor and frequent speaker on men's issues and is Professor of Pastoral Theology at Seminary of the East in Dresher, Pennsylvania. He was a contributor to *Husbands and Wives*, published by Scripture Press, and has written articles for *Christian Herald, Christian Education Today, Christian Reader*, and other magazines. He also writes *Men's Memo*, a bimonthly devotional letter for Christian men.

Robert Hicks articles appear on pages 136 and 154 and are reprinted from *Uneasy Manhood* by Robert Hicks, published by Oliver-Nelson Publishers.

Bill Hybels is pastor of Willow Creek Community Church, which reaches out to the unchurched in the Chicago area. It has grown from 125 people to over 9,000 is just a decade. He is an author and speaker. His articles on pages 60 and 216 come from *Who You Are When No One's Looking* by Bill Hybels, ©1987 by Bill Hybels. Used by permission of InterVarsity Press, P.O. Box 1400, Downers Grove, IL 60515.

Jerry B. Jenkins is the author of over eighty books. He and his wife, Dianna, and their sons live at Three-Son Acres, west of Zion, Illinois. The article on page 102 is taken from *Lessons Learned Early* by Jerry Jenkins. Copyright 1991 Moody Bible Institute of Chicago, Moody Press. Used by permission.

Tim Kimmel and his wife, Darcy, have three children and live in Phoenix, Arizona. As president of Generation Ministries, Tim speaks on family issues to thousands of young people, parents, and military personnel throughout the United States and Canada. Tim is the author of *The Little House on the Freeway* and *Legacy of Love*. His article is located on page 134.

Andrew T. LePeau is editorial director at InterVarsity Press and with his wife, Phyllis, has written extensively on family issues. His articles are found on pages 50 and 146.

Bill McCartney is the head football coach of the University of Colorado Buffaloes. He is also an author and the founder of Promise Keepers. His articles are found on pages 9 and 233.

Udo Middelman was born in Germany and educated in Germany, the United States, and Switzerland. He holds a degree in law from Freiburg University and a B.D. and M.A. from Covenant Seminary in St. Louis. He is professor of Philosophy and Theology at King's College and director/president of the Francis Schaeffer Foundation in Briarcliffe Manor, New York. His articles are found on 196, 200, and 217.

Chuck Miller is an educator/pastor in the areas of leadership development, parenting, and discipling. He is currently serving on the faculties of Azusa Pacific University and the Leadership Institute, teaching in the area of leadership. Chuck Miller's articles are found on pages 106, 130, 174, and 180.

Dr. Gary Oliver is the clinical director of Southwest Counseling Associates, as well as an author and speaker. His articles are found on pages 26 and 176.

Don Osgood—After being with IBM for thirty years, Don Osgood started the Career Performance Group, which hosts motivational seminars. Mr. Osgood is also an author and the excerpt, beginning on page 95, is used with his permission.

Luis Palau is a noted author and international evangelist who has preached and taught to over 9,000,000 people around the world. His articles appear on pages 34, 152, 194, and 198.

Roger Palms is the editor of *Decision* magazine and the author of numerous books, including *Enjoying the Closeness of God*. His article appears on page 32.

Dennis Rainey is the national director of the Family Ministry of Campus Crusade for Christ International and has appeared before Congress on behalf of the family. He is the author of *Lonely Husbands, Lonely Wives*, among other titles. His articles appear on pages 78 and 214.

Bill Sanders conducts his seminars in 150 public schools per year. He is the author of *Life, Sex, and Everything in Between,* as well as other titles, including his most recent *School Daze.* His article appears on page 54.

Fran Sciacca is a high-school teacher with a tremendous sensitivity for his students and the problems they face. He is the author of *Wounded Saints, Generation at Risk,* and the best-selling Bible study *To Walk and Not Grow Weary.* His articles appear on pages 104 and 222.

Dave Simmons is founder and director of Dad, The Family Shepherd Ministries. Tens of thousands of men have attended his seminars seeking to be better dads to their sons. The article on page 114 is adapted from *Dad the Family Coach* by Dave Simmons, published by Victor Books ©1977, Scripture Press Publications, Wheaton, IL 60187.

Gary Smalley is president of Today's Family and speaks extensively throughout the world. With John Trent, his writings, such as *The Language of Love* and *The Blessing,* have sold in the millions. Their articles appear on pages 15, 29, 39, 61, 83, 109, 125, 141, 157, 173, 183, 203, and 225.

Dr. Charles F. Stanley is the pastor of the historic First Baptist Church of Atlanta and the author of numerous books, including *How to Listen to God.* The article on page 82 is reprinted from *A Man's Touch* by Charles Stanley, published by Victor Books © 1977, Scripture Press Publications, Wheaton, IL 60187.

Kenneth Taylor is a Bible translator and author. He is the founder and chairman of the board of Tyndale House Publishers. In addition to *The Living Bible,* he has written more than twenty books. The article on page 69 is from *My Life: A Guided Tour* by Ken Taylor ©1992. Used by permission of Tyndale House Publishers, Inc. All rights reserved.

Dr. John Trent, Ph.D., is vice president of Today's Family. With Gary Smalley, his writings, such as *The Language of Love* and *The Blessing,* have sold in the millions. Their articles appear on pages 15, 29, 39, 61, 83, 109, 125, 141, 157, 173, 183, 203, and 225.

Dr. Jerry White is the general director of The Navigators. He is the author of *The Power of Commitment,* published by The Navigators of Singapore, 1990. U.S. Distributor: Glen Eyrie Bookstore, The Navigators, P.O. Box 6000, Colorado Springs, CO 80934. His article appears on page 143.

John Yates is the rector of the Falls Church Episcopal Church in Falls Church, Virginia. He is a speaker and author, and his most recent book is cowritten with his wife, Susan, from Word Books entitled *What Really Matters at Home.* His articles appear on pages 36 and 72.

Promise Keepers: The Ministry

Randy Phillips, Executive Director of Promise Keepers

W hen the idea for this book first saw the light of day, we were hoping that it would be a "conference in print." We wanted this book to be as encouraging and challenging to men as the Promise Keeper's conferences have been to those of us in the Colorado area who first started gathering together.

Yet nothing takes the place of men gathering together and fellowshiping one with another. Perhaps you would consider joining with other men to help each other be promise keepers.

Promise Keepers seeks to be a supply line to the local church, helping to encourage and assist pastors and ministry leaders in calling men to an accountable relationship with Jesus Christ and with one another. Promise Keeper's wants to provide men's material (like this book) as well as seminars and an annual conference to emphasizes the godly conviction, integrity, and action each of us needs.

Please join us in helping one another be the kind of men God wants us to be. Write or call our offices today.

Promise Keepers
P.O. Box 18376
Boulder, CO 80308
(303) 421-2800